God
Turned
Toward Us

Will Willimon

God Turned Toward Us

The ABCs of Christian Faith

Abingdon Press

Nashville

GOD TURNED TOWARD US:
THE ABCS OF CHRISTIAN FAITH

Copyright © 2021 by Will Willimon

ISBN: 9781791018894

Library of Congress Control Number: 2021937842

21 22 23 24 25 26 27 28 29 30 31—10 9 8 7 6 5 4 3 2 1
MANUFACTURED IN THE UNITED STATES OF AMERICA

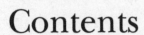

Contents

Contents

Contents

Contents

Preface

As great a challenge as walking with Christ is talking his walk. So Jesus's disciples pled, "Lord, teach us!" Give us the words to speak to God.

Some faiths may arise from your sweet subjectivity, accompany your birth, occur after secluded meditation, as fruit of walks in the woods, discoveries from human experience, good and bad, or what you've learned from your wounds. Christianity isn't one of them.

Nobody is born believing that God is a Jew from Nazareth who lived briefly, died violently, rose unexpectedly, and resumed speaking to those who betrayed him. Somebody must give us words that open the doors into the faith called Christian. In submitting to God's talk to us—allowing ourselves to be addressed by the God we're unable to love without first being loved, incapable of discovering without being found, inept to speak to without being addressed—God apprehends us. While we were struggling to get our minds around God, surprise: God already had us in mind. Striving to be spiritual—to think, feel, or act rightly, hefting ourselves out of hemmed in humanity—God turned toward us.

No mere projection from either human insecurity or arrogance, knowledge of Christ is not had because we want it. Divine/human conversation is at God's instigation, God's initiative, that is, grace: unmerited, unearned, gift of the testimony of the saints, living and dead, an ancient text that talks today, a Sunday sermon that the Holy Spirit commandeered to speak to you, especially you.

The truth about God comes our way through God's refusal to give up on divine/human colloquy and abandon us to soliloquy. For good reason is Jesus "The Word." Whoever said, "I'd rather see a sermon than hear one," or "Preach the gospel at all times. If necessary, use words," it wasn't Jesus.

Only God talks us into God and, in Jesus Christ, surprise, God does. The God afforded in scripture is loquacious, ubiquitous, a revealing, determined conversationalist who revels not only in being God but also in telling us all about it. Christian language is no more odd or difficult than it has to be in order accurately to describe the God who turns to us as Christ.

"Young man, watch your language," was an admonition I heard as an adolescent. Christians must mind the words we use. Want to be a Christian? You'll have to learn the vocabulary and walk the walk that enable these words to make sense. Inarticulacy is no virtue. Once God in Christ turned toward us, self-disclosed, we were forced, like Saul-become-Paul, to radically redefine words like *slave*, *love*, or *redemption*.

Preachers are stewards of our sacred speech, always remembering that Christian words are known, not by definitions in a book but by living in the world, not by explanation and interpretation but by active walking with the Word who gives us words that show we know what we are talking about when we say "God." If you've been a parent who's taught a child to speak English, or if you've done time as a teacher of high school French, pounding French verbs into the heads of recalcitrant youth, it's no wonder that God has called you to be a curator of Christian speech.

You may want to use this book devotionally, reading an entry each day. At the end of this book I've included **"Pathways to Follow"** for preachers and teachers looking for ways to communicate the gospel to their congregations, and for individuals and groups, in church and out, pursuing themes and trajectories related to the

Christian faith. In the **"Notes"** section are the biblical texts on which my assertions are based, showing my attempt to demonstrate my desire to be unoriginal.

Let's celebrate the words whereby the church teaches us to live with the God who talks to us. God refusing to be confined in divinity, divinity dwindled to infancy, God we would never have made up for ourselves giving us the words for thoughts and lives we would have missed had not God turned toward us.

Will Willimon

ABORTION

A word (found nowhere in the Bible) for a medical procedure performed solely on pregnant women.

Half of American Christians think abortion is very wrong because life is a right; half think it regrettable, though sometimes permissible if freely chosen by the woman. Neither group musters much theological support; their positions say more about their obeisance to the political left or right than their obedience to scripture. Life is a gift, not a "right"; freedom of choice is an American rather than a Christian fetish. Limit your thought to the world's vocabulary, and end up with nothing better than the world's solutions.

While early Christians scandalized imperial Romans by condemning infant exposure (the killing of unwanted babies)—along with refusing emperor worship and military service—they would have been baffled by Christians who brag about their commitment to "the sanctity of life" while supporting policies that make children the poorest of all Americans and put immigrant kids in cages.

Christians work through argument, persuasion, and conversion, not by seizing political power to cram our way down everyone else's throat. Unwilling to take time to persuade, opponents of abortion-on-demand demand government punishment of women, sidling up to politicians who promised, through judicial coercion, to compel behavior that they couldn't achieve in their own congregations. Advocates of abortion as a right demand that the government protect and care for women rather than work justice in their own congregations by showing the world how Christ wants us to treat the powerless and vulnerable.

1

Better than schemes for legislative compulsion would be for us to create the sort of churches where women are not left to make and to live with tough choices on their own and are, through the generous support of fellow Christians, enabled to receive the gift of new life as God gives it. Church ought to be the one place where we take responsibility for children who are not our own, a practice otherwise known as baptism.

While destruction of life is a sin, making abortion the one and only concern of the church, an excuse to egg on sleazy politicians or to impugn the faith of fellow Christians is no virtue.

APOCALYPTIC

Unveil, reveal, also end, or begin.

Biblical books like Daniel, Ezekiel, and most memorably, the Revelation to John, are "apocalyptic." Horned beasts, night visions, dry bones taking on flesh are weird talk, even for scripture. Apocalyptic language is no odder than it needs to be, not to obscure and keep secret but to unveil and reveal. When God at last turns toward us, what God's up to is so beyond the scope of our expectation that only rich, metaphorical, unmanageable speech will do.

Apocalyptic keeps Christians maladjusted to the present. Yes, Daniel's visions speak of the future but also make claims about the now. Don't be fooled by the seeming solidity of the contemporary. God has more things up God's sleeve.

Powerful, privileged people get nervous when the talk turns apocalyptic. Urbane dismissal of this futuristic literature that tilts toward a new heaven and earth is a sign of our ease in Zion. This world is as good as it gets; work it to your advantage and privilege. The Christian faith is a primitive technique for holding onto what you've got. Stop whining; cease dreaming. Content yourself with things as they are. Steady, upward progress is easier on the psyche than abrupt killing of the old and birth of the new. Keep disruptive visions to yourself.

The nightmarish apparitions of Daniel said little to me. Then came COVID-19, the body counts tallied in the daily news, impotent old men refusing to vacate high places, trouble in the streets, and people cowering behind locked doors for fear. The penny dropped.

Whenever people dare think, "We are slaves, slaves in the land that you gave to our ancestors," the soothing reassurances of mainline liberal preaching wilt. Whenever someone takes seriously, "Don't be conformed to this world! Be transformed by the blowing of your mind!" nothing less than eerie visions of a divinely renovated heaven and earth will do.

Apocalyptic takes evil seriously, God's agency even more so. If things are set right between us and God, God must do it. The solution will be cosmic, not merely personal. Should God be turning toward us, there are sure to be jolts and bumps. Something must die in order for anything to be born.

The Old Testament saves apocalyptic until the end. In the New Testament, from the get-go, from Mary's song, it's new heaven and new earth, world turned upside down, the rise and fall of many. Bad news for the rich, good news for the poor and dispossessed.

Just before Jesus gets to his cross, he waxes apocalyptic, suggesting that the cross means more than only the good die young; Calvary is a world all shook up, God's cosmic, decisive, "No!" to our death and sin, "Yes!" to our future with God.

What can we expect of God? A homeowner sleeps, secure in his stuff. During the night, he awakes; a thief has broken in and ripped off everything. Jesus warns us to live as if all we think is ours, safe, and sound, is about to get ripped off. Losers, wake-up!

God the thief, the great rip off, not the most flattering divine image, to be sure. Good news or bad? Much depends on how tightly you're holding on to the stuff you've got.

Jesus apocalyptically strides in as the new and the now, announcing that God is launching a great invasion to take back what belongs to God. Others had talked about the advent of God's kingdom. Jesus announces it as now. A whole new world breaking into the old. Stretching out his arms on the cross, he brings down the whole rickety apparatus of empire. Striding forth from the tomb, the earth shook.

Apocalyptic refuses to use God as the cement of social conformity or to reduce the gospel to common sense. Button-down establishment Christianity has always been nervous about Jesus's apocalyptic talk. Those of us at the top find the gospel easier when it's toned down to sooth the anxious consciences of us who benefit from things as they are. But to those on the bottom or at the margins who are paralyzed and hopeless from fear that their existence is as good as it gets, apocalyptic is good news.

Apocalyptic says that God's creativity doesn't end at Genesis; dismantling and disruption presage new creation. God will get what God wants: bad news for those of us tightly wedded to and profiting from the present, good news for those in need of a different future.

The deistic God of the philosophers, a minimalist, inactive, unobtrusive, noninvasive, unrevealing God is about as much of God as we moderns can take. Jesus the teacher of morality, a really nice person who loved lilies and was kind to children and people with disabilities.

No, says apocalyptic. He is a peripatetic, wild Jew from Nazareth who won't stay confined within our boundaries for God. He comes to cast fire on the earth, tear apart families, topple kingdoms, and thereby offer us a refashioned world we could never create by ourselves.

Even though Jesus warned us against speculation on a timeline for God's promised apocalypse, down through the years, many have been disappointed that God doesn't work on our schedule. Maybe, since Jesus's advent, any time God turns to us and we see ending and beginning, it's apocalypse.

Amid the demonstrations of the Black Lives Matter movement, white politicians promised a return to "law and order." During the height of the pandemic, many said, "Can't wait for the world to get back to normal." Christians, fed on apocalyptic expectation of God's coming reign, hungry for more, say "God, we hope not."

ASS

A profane beast of burden who gained enigmatic theological significance once God became incarnate in Jesus Christ, and the exaltedly spiritual got down and dirty.

Jacob called his son Issachar a "strong ass," perhaps as a term of endearment. Using only a donkey's jawbone, Samson slayed a thousand Philistines. Our pastor treasured Job 1:14: "The oxen were plowing, and the asses were grazing," which he interpreted as a parable of how our ox-like pastor worked tirelessly for the Lord, unlike recumbent, asinine laity.

We are prohibited from coveting our neighbor's ass. Job boasted "five hundred she asses"only to lose them as collateral damage in a wager between the Satan and the Lord. After Job's tribulations ended, the Lord blessed Job with a thousand. Thus began the prosperity gospel with its well-heeled preachers.

God looks at donkeys differently than we do. For dozens of chapters Job cries, "Why did these terrible things happen to me?" At last God shows up answering, not with theodicy—justifying God's ways to humanity—but with swaggering braggadocio:

5

Who freed the wild donkey . . . ?
He laughs at the clamor of the town,
doesn't hear the driver's shout.

Maybe the wild-at-heart ass knows he's one of God's favorites as
he gleefully ignores commands and, looking upon the oh-so-serious
human "clamor of the town," laughs, "hee-haw."

The most famous biblical ass is Balaam's. Bearing Balaam down
a road, the ass abruptly stopped. Balaam, looking like a fool who
couldn't control his donkey, whopped the ass. The donkey, terri-
fied by his vision of a sword-wielding divine messenger, squeezed
Balaam's foot against the wall. Balaam furiously thrashed his ass.
"Hey! What have I done that you've beaten me these three times?"
retorted the ass.

Balaam fumed, "If I had a sword, I'd kill you."

To which the donkey countered in perfect Hebrew, "You have
ridden on my back all day and have I ever complained?"

Then the divine messenger interrupted the ass-versus-prophet
quarrel by asking Balaam, "Why have you beaten your donkey? It
was I who blocked the road. Your donkey saw what you couldn't see
and tried three times to protect you by turning away. I oughta kill
you—you myopic, ass of a prophet—and let your donkey live."

Laity love this story. Sit through enough sermons, sooner or later
you'll hear God speak through a jackass.

Although Christmas cards picture the Holy Family arriving at
Bethlehem and then escaping to Egypt by way of a donkey, there's no
mention of it in the Gospels. No asses until Jesus's climactic last week
when Zechariah gives Israel the good news that the king is coming:

See, your king comes to you,
righteous and victorious,
lowly and riding on a donkey,
on a colt, the foal of a donkey.

6

King Jesus bounces in on the back of a fuzzy donkey, welcomed not by the city's bigwigs but rather by a gaggle of kids waving palm branches?

The drama of Holy Week begins with the mundane details of renting of a donkey.

When the owner of the donkey sees the disciples untying his donkey, he asks, "What the heck are you doing?"

"The master needs it," they reply.

We hear no more of the donkey that played a key role in the opening act of the passion. Maybe that's the way it is with us fuzzy disciples who obey the Lord, playing our bit parts in the drama of salvation, then bouncing off into obscurity, remembered only by the Lord who condescends to need us, even us.

Few can aspire to the sanctity of an Augustine or a Theresa, but most of us can hope to be the beasts who bear our Lord into the city, playing our bit part in his grand pageant of salvation, grateful for a Savior who, for all his glory, stoops to utilize asses like us.

ATHEISM

The determination not to believe in the God who, in Jesus Christ, believes in us.

Scripture's question is not, "Is there a God?" but "Who is the God who is?" Far from being the end of a lonely journey through tortured intellectual questions and doubts, contemporary atheism is a byproduct of the modern penchant for knowing more and more about less and less, reality dumbed down to that which can be explained without God. Close your eyes and try hard to believe that there's nothing afoot, no beyond.

Once God chose not to have us through coercion, disbelief became a real possibility. Even though Jesus said that whoever sees him "has seen the Father," we're part of the crowd who "seeing, do not see."

Back in the nineteenth century, atheism required intellectual grit; now godlessness is the conventional position of anybody who's too proud to stoop to belief in a God who would stoop to love losers like us.

Before you distain atheistic rejection of the gospel, consider how the world's disbelief is parasitic on our flabby believing. Establishment Christianity gives atheists less and less to disbelieve. Evangelicals shot themselves in the foot with their GOP right-wing politics; trendier-than-thou progressives became the Democratic Party at prayer. Thus have millions mistaken their belief that "the church is silly and superficial" for disbelief in God.

Dangers abound for the determined atheist. Reality is manifold, murky, and miscellaneous. That's why most people looking at "what is" suspect someone must be behind it. If God really is Jesus Christ, reconciling the world to himself, successfully fending off divine hints, overtures and flirtations can be a full-time job. More than a PhD in philosophy is required to keep God off your back.

Christian, be fair. Consider what we are asking the world to wrap its head around: infinity inhabiting a finite man, a virgin who is a mother, a baby born into the world he created, a God who help-lessly dies, a dead man who lives, he who had everything submitting to life as a beggar, the one who had all power refusing to raise his hand against his killers, the best person who ever lived become the victim of the worst of human cruelty.

When people say they don't believe in God, there's a good chance that they are disbelieving in some God proxy who has been presented to them as the real thing. Ask them, "Who is the God in whom you don't believe?" Nine times out of ten you will be able to say, "Wonderful! I don't believe in that God either."

Atheists usually define themselves on the basis of what they don't believe, lacking self-awareness that their vaunted disbelief is based upon their rigid, closed-minded belief in something rather than nothing. Their problem is not that they don't believe in God but that they have put way too much faith in some god substitute of the moment. Thus a fitting response to the atheist's "I don't believe in anything" is "I don't believe you."

ATONEMENT

At-one-ment. Christ refusing to reign in heaven without us. All the ways God has taken sole responsibility for setting matters right between us and God, primarily in the cross of Christ.

Atonement (from a Hebrew word translated by the Common English Bible as "reconciliation") is God turning, coming alongside, overcoming separation due to human sin. God, who could have punished, electing instead to forgive. God determined to be Emmanuel, God-with-Us even unto death.

Who is God? What's God up to? Nine out of ten will say that God is large, up there, out there, aloof. God the judge who sets high a moral bar we will never chin up to. God the creator who messed up by creating us and now puts as much distance as possible between us disappointing creatures and God's high and mighty divinity.

The Christian doctrine of the atonement says otherwise. Though from the first we turned away from God every chance we got—our pride, lust, idolatry, injustice, and smart-mouthed sin are well documented—God turned toward us. Relentlessly redemptive Yahweh made covenant with us, gave the Ten Commandments, sent the prophets to tell the truth we dared not tell ourselves, created a family out of two geriatrics to bless all the world's families, sent us one to substitute for us, to suffer, and to die for us, ransom us, pay for our sin, be the slaughtered lamb who reigns, stomp down death by rising from the dead and returning to us with holes in his hands and a wound in his side. God in action.

It's not only who Jesus is but also what he has done that makes the difference. "It is finished." Atonement is his completed work to which we need add nothing. "Christ died for our sins," "Jesus paid it all," "we've been saved," "brought from death to life," "he bore our curse," truth so deep that it takes a dizzying array of metaphors to talk about it—and still there is much left unsaid.

"I'd do anything for my children," we parents often say. When God said it, God meant it; God did it. Any God who is determined to reconnect, reconcile, and redeem people like us must not be squeamish about shedding blood, for we have a long history of murdering our saviors. Love hurts. God loves us to death.

> When God our savior's kindness and love appeared, he saved us because of his mercy, not because of righteous things we had done. He did it through the washing of new birth and the renewing by the Holy Spirit, which God poured out upon us generously through Jesus Christ our savior.

From the first, Christians said, "Christ died for our sin." Yet atonement is not simply a transaction whereby Jesus paid our debt. Jesus is more than a divine afterthought, that is, God's plan B after our sin messed up God's plan A. As Paul says, Christ, in his death and resurrection is the "kindness and love" of God, what God was doing all along. Or as one of the church fathers put it, even if we hadn't sinned, God would have still come for us.

After his cross and resurrection, Jesus's people raced throughout the world with good news that "God raised crucified Jesus from the dead!" Naturally, somebody asked, "Who has been raised from the dead? What did he say? What did he do?" The next question was, "What's the meaning of what has happened in Christ?" Thus was Christian theology born as Christians' answers to the world's questions. God was in Christ, in his crucifixion and resurrection, doing much the same atoning work as in the creation of the world, or in the exodus of Israel out of enslavement.

Somehow, someway, as Paul preached, "God was reconciling the world to himself through Christ, by not counting people's sins against them." That's the mystery of at-one-ment, God dealing decisively with our self-distancing from God.

Welcome to the revolution.

BAPTISM

Christian initiation.

When you join Rotary, you get a lapel pin, a handshake, and lunch. When you are initiated into the body of Christ, we strip you down, bathe you, half drown you, pull you up all wet and sticky like a newborn, lay hands on your head, give you a job way beyond your natural abilities, and call you by the name Christian.

Don't say you weren't warned.

Baptism means what water means: refreshment, fun, birth, life, death, all in the name of the Father, Son, and Holy Spirit. Baptism is something done to you rather than by you, just like your salvation, which may account for why the church has rarely troubled itself over the age or qualifications of baptism's recipients. As a sacrament, baptism is a gift of God whereby God—knowing that we are animals—uses the ordinary, bodily, stuff of mundane creaturely life to get through to us, to signify God turned toward us in ways that we can comprehend.

Nobody is born Christian. Water + the story of Jesus + God rewriting your story + your willingness to be written into the story of Jesus = Christian. You are not the sole author of the narrative of your life. God has not left up to you the burden of crafting your significance. How much did you contribute to your first birth? You don't have to struggle to figure out who you are or what you ought to be doing with whatever years you've got; in baptism, the church tells you.

Without much debate, the church baptized the children of Christian parents, promising God we would bring up children as if they were Christians. To be sure, it's absurd to call a little baby, squalling and indignant, "Christian." Yet that's just what the church does until, sooner or later, the promises of baptism are fulfilled; we have become that person who the church promised we would be. Somebody calls out, "Christian," and we answer because, by the grace of God, the name fits.

It's a comfort—particularly during rough times—to know that, in baptism, God has taken full responsibility for your salvation. Even though we don't always think like Christians, much less act like it, by baptism God promises to go ahead and be our God anyway. Even though you are sometimes most unlovable and unbearable, the church, by baptism, promises to put up with you to the end, relighting the baptism candle, posting it by your coffin, as we give you back to the God who gave you to us.

In baptism, the old sinful Adam is put to death. Yet, as Martin Luther noted, the Old Adam is a mighty good swimmer. Every day you wake up, jump out of bed, and submit to the continuing work begun in your baptism. Though the rite of baptism takes only a few minutes to perform, it takes your whole life to finish what was begun in you when the church doused you "in the name of the Father, the Son, and the Holy Spirit" and called you Christian.

BEELZEBUB

AKA Satan, Devil, Lucifer, Prince of Darkness, Prince of Demons, The Strong Man, The Ruler of the Air, The Ruler of This World. When dressed

*in blue, the Duke University mascot. "Beelzebub" may have been a play
on the name of a Canaanite god, Lord of Flies. Flies are born in and eat
excrement, which suggests that Satan is never to be taken too seriously.*

Little is heard from the Satan (the accuser) in the Old Testament. Back in the day, when God and Satan were on speaking terms, the Satan, source of evil, sends a series of calamities to afflict Job. (However evil got here, it's not from God.) Without implicating the Satan, the psalmist says that humanity's thoughts are evil since junior high. We all like sheep quite gleefully have gone astray without need of satanic prompting. What's wrong with the world? Mostly me.

When Jesus shows up on the scene, the strong man stirs. Preparing for his ministry, not with three years of seminary but with a lonely forty-day fast in the wilderness, Jesus is jumped by Satan. "If you are the Son of God (which the voice at your baptism proclaimed you to be) then act like it," said Satan, offering the lonely, famished young rabbi three tempting alternatives: turn stones to bread (think of the hungry people you could feed with that trick), take charge of "all the kingdoms of this world" because "they have been given to me" (whose bright idea was it to turn politics and government over to Satan?), and "throw yourself off the tip of the temple" (EWTN will make you a star). To Satan's inducements, Jesus says "No!," determined to be the messiah he is rather than the savior we craved.

Satan slinks away, lying in wait until "a more acceptable time."

Jesus's critics accused him of casting out demons by the power of Beelzebul. "Driving out Satan by Satan?" scoffed Jesus. No. "God's kingdom has already overtaken you." By signs and wonders, Jesus signified his reclamation of enemy-held territory. Maybe that's why demons first recognized Jesus's identity. Cruel King Herod (shaking in his boots when Jesus was born) was the first to see the political peril presented by Jesus.

Scripture doesn't tell us from whence evil came but tells us how God responds to the evil that's there. Jesus made clear his intention to go head-to-head with evil personified, declaring, on his way to the cross, "Now this world's ruler will be thrown out," predicting that when hoisted up, he would defeat Satan by magnetically drawing all to himself, robbing Satan of his prey.

If you've never experienced evil organized, resourceful, and dangerous, you may think you are too sophisticated to believe in the possibility of Satan. But the persistence, subtlety, and intractability of white racism is more than a psychological inclination, a glitch in our education; it's satanic. Impersonal explanations like "white privilege," or "structural racism" don't quite match the depth of our evil. Beelzebub!

God's creations are good, so the church has traditionally seen Satan as a prime example of God's good intentions thwarted, though to say that God "created" Satan is no more correct than to speak of a mirror that was created to be broken.

Why has God not made a world without evil? Because it wouldn't be a world with you.

Satan masquerades as an angel of light. Gathering with his closest friends for a last supper, Jesus noted Satan among them. Looking for the satanic? Look first in the church.

Still, the church is wise not to give the devil his due. "The devil made me do it" can be an evasion of responsibility. More troubling, to speak too seriously of Satan is to cast aspersions on Jesus's reign. Is Christ busy reconciling the world to himself or not? It's okay to be curious about Satan but not overly so; the devil is defeated, rendered impotent, lord of nothing, present, painful, yes, but ultimately unreal and inconsequential.

We don't need to mythologize or personalize evil; it's on the evening news as a white policeman's knee on George Floyd's neck. Lord Jesus may have defeated the Lord of the Flies but, for the time being, gives him/her/they/it a long leash. I'm unsure just how God is going to sort it all out. Still, if Jesus Christ is Lord and Satan's minions are not, then it's hard to imagine that anybody, even Beelzebub, can forever withstand the transformation that God wants to work throughout the still groaning cosmos.

The line between good and evil is not between God and Satan; it runs through each human heart. So if you really must waste time pondering the old Lord of the Flies, then worry about Beelzebub leveraging your loneliness, hunger, ambitiousness, resentfulness, and pride rather than your neighbor's. Label your enemy as coworker with Satan, arm yourself for combat to set the world right through your virtuous crusade; Satan grins, "Gotcha!"

As Jesus hung from his cross, Satan at last finds his "more acceptable time" to show up and take charge. The democratic mob mocks Jesus, "If you are the Son of God, act like it. Throw yourself down from the cross." Satan need say nothing at Golgotha; there, at the foot of the cross, Satan's words are on our lips.

BIBLE

Scripture. Revelation. The library of God's word.

Why God has chosen to turn toward humanity primarily through this rather disordered collection of books, written in languages and arising out of cultures so different from our own, God only knows. Millions have found that though scripture is the product of flawed, limited, frail human beings, the Trinity ventures speech through the Bible anyway.

Reading the Bible became difficult in modern times—not because we're critical, scientific, and sophisticated but because we lost the skills of reading literature as thick, multifaceted, and demanding as the Bible. The God of Israel and the church refuses to be limited to a single voice or one historical period. Saga, stories, parables, laws, genealogies, history, poetry, the God of the Bible has quite a rhetorical repertoire. It takes all of four Gospels to talk about the one God in Christ. Not even a voice as richly ranged as Isaiah's could do justice to the full range of God's loquaciousness.

An even greater challenge in reading the Bible and getting anything out of it is that it's not just literature; it's scripture—a story about God written by God, God speaking to modern people who don't expect to be addressed other than by our own dear little voice within.

"The Bible says" has been supplanted by, "In my personal experience." The external word from scripture squelched by the imperialism of the subjective, the dumb certitude of thinking that what's happened to us equals divine revelation.

The Bible sounds dull and irrelevant because it's not about you and you have been trained to care mostly about you. "Where am I in this ancient story?" God only knows.

Scripture is God unveiling God. Don't start with a definition of God and then rummage about in the Bible for validation. Comprehending scripture is no more difficult than it has to be, considering the Bible's subject. That's why Sunday mornings don't usually get out of hand until this big book is opened, read, and preached.

Readers may be put off occasionally by the Bible's intention to be the most honest book you'll ever read. The Bible is about God's love, restoration, and creation, but along the way it tells the unvarnished truth about human betrayal, hate, chaos, and violence. Here is humanity undisguised. Sure, there's a heap of blood-letting and head-bashing in the Bible—some human, some divine. But it's bad taste for the people who slaughtered Native Americans, produced and defended enslavement of Africans, and dropped the bomb on Hiroshima to shed crocodile tears for the Canaanites.

Scripture wants not just to inform but to convert. As a rule of thumb, if you read a passage and say "Yep, that's what I always thought," read it again. The truth that the Bible speaks doesn't arise from any human heart. That's why we call it a "passage of scripture;" to enter the strange, new world of the Bible is to dare venture into a foreign land that you can't get to without the Bible taking you there.

The Bible has a privileged place in Christian communication. Through centuries of trial and error, Israel and the church have found its testimony to be trustworthy. We are not free, as the church, to rummage among other authorities, sources of inspiration, and revelation until we have first submitted to scripture, saying as little Samuel, "Speak, Lord, your servant is listening."

No congregation says, "Preacher, since you are a life expert, dole out some good advice on how to make it through the week." Rather, the question put to preachers is, "Any word from the Lord?" Thus a good interpretive principle: "The Bible always and everywhere speaks primarily about God and only secondarily or derivatively talks about us."

The Bible pressures us to perform, enact, and embody its message. In diverse, sly ways, scripture asks more than the cerebral, "Do you understand?" Scripture's word is the political, "Come, join up." If the church had been a seminar to study ancient sayings of Jesus, Caesar would have never noticed.

Second Timothy states that "Every scripture is inspired by God and is useful for teaching, for showing mistakes, for correcting, and for training character," which sounds like the Bible is a rulebook for doctrinal policing, but then the writer adds, "so that the person who belongs to God can be equipped to do everything that is good." Enlistment rather than agreement is the Bible's goal.

Infallible? Only to the extent that God will infallibly say whatever God wants.

God doesn't dictate scripture (or much of anything else). Rather, God allows human witnesses and their words to become God's word. We privilege these ancient witnesses (no easy task for moderns who have progressed to the summit of human development—Durham, North Carolina, 2021). We trust those who were closest to Jesus, particularly those who paid in blood, dying for the stories they had been told.

Harriet Tubman read Exodus and thought it was talking about her and her enslaved people, so much so that she got nicknamed Moses.

The temptation, in interpreting scripture, lies in our tendency to come across some biblical passage, find it odd, and say, "How can I make this passage relevant to my life?" The Bible has bolder goals: to make your life relevant to scripture. Refusing to take your meager, modern assessment of reality too seriously, the Bible wants to rock your world. Unwilling to let the present moment dictate its significance, scripture lifts your eyes above the merely contemporary. Thus a lifetime of reading and listening is required to take scripture a bit more seriously and ourselves a little less so.

The Bible wasn't meant to be read solo. Get help from some commentators who have given their lives to the ministry of interpretation. Find a congregation who gathers in order to bend their lives toward the Word. It takes at least two to make sense of scripture: one to assert what one hears in a passage and another to expand the other's hearing. No, three are required. Only by the intervention of Holy Spirit will scripture say wonderful things to you that you would never say to yourself.

The Bible is a window through which we are given a privileged peek into the heart of God. As with any window, sometimes the glass we're looking through becomes a mirror whereby we see an image of ourselves reflected by the pane. Don't let a commentary distract you with too many details by turning what's meant to be a telescope into a microscope.

Scripture is deeply historical: God speaks and reveals through thoroughly human words in time. Trouble is,

1. More is going on in human history than human history.
2. The resurrection is an event in history that, by its very nature overturns human history. Scriptural texts do more than reportage; they preach, reveal, detoxify, and recruit.

Don't worry too much about the historical context of a biblical passage, as if the time between us and the text were our greatest challenge. Biblical scholars don't know as much about the originating context as they sometimes claim. Your greatest concern is not to speculate on what God said back then as to have the guts to be open to what God might be saying to you right now. The scholar who says, "Jesus couldn't have said this" is usually showing a lack of imagination, a refusal to allow God to act in ways that are beyond the limited expectation of somebody with a PhD in biblical studies.

Still, read with confidence that God really does want to implicate you. Seek and you will find. There you are, just listening to one of the Bible's weird stories, feeling safe, thinking that you have successfully defended yourself against its grasp, bored by a story about some Jew named Joseph and his hyperdysfunctional family (few happy families in scripture), wondering why God could have bet the farm on such losers, only to exclaim, "Hey! Are you talking about me?" Jolted and jostled, wandering in a strange world you did not concoct for yourself, addressed by this ancient text, you'll know why the Bible has been called a God-breathed book that talks.

Remember that God wants us to succeed at biblical interpretation and application: "These things are written." Why? "That you might believe."

BODY

Gift of God. Temple for God's glorification. What God assumed out of God's determination to turn to us where we are, as we are. Source of much human pain and anguish and also some of our greatest fun.

Our bodies remind us that we are animals. In one creation account God makes our bodies from mud, then loans us breath. Fairly early we begin our trek back to the earth from which we came. Mortality is not an injustice; it's who we are. Cosmetics and workouts sometimes slow but never stop our downward descent back to dirt.

Bodies can be the hard part of being human. Therefore, Paul speaks of our groaning as we await the "redemption of our bodies." Only the God who created bodies can help us with them; therefore a huge amount of prayer is expended on carnal, bodily deterioration.

We are inseparably *psyche* and *soma*. Even in his resurrection, Christ had a body. When some of his disciples failed to recognize him in his resurrected body, he showed them the holes in his hands, the wound in his side, and ate some leftover fish. Seeing is believing. Bodily proof is irrefutable. That's Jesus. He remembers that we are bodies who sometimes need tangible, visible evidence in order to believe. Thus we come to church, a piece of bread is placed in our hands with the words, "The *body* of Christ, given for you."

As someone who writes books, I'm embarrassed that Jesus never had the need to publish anything. He left us no constitution, set of ethical guidelines, nor founding document. His body is his primary way of revealing himself to the world and bringing the world to himself. Christ's body, the church, the way Christ takes up room, his visible, corporeal presence, physical proof of his reign.

To be sure, believing that your congregation, with all its flaws and failings, is the body of Christ requires a leap of faith. It's a heck of a way for Christ to be in the world. Still, it's his way of refusing to allow us to dismiss him as an apolitical, disincarnate, spiritual blur.

BOREDOM

The bored look upon God's world, God's gifts, and yawn, "That's all you've got to show me?"

Danish Christian philosopher Kierkegaard says that boredom leads to much of our sin. We grab hold of anything in a vain attempt to make our lives mean something.

Though not a biblical sin, boredom, especially when committed by preachers, is an offense against the Holy Spirit who promises to liven up even the most tedious sermon or lackluster congregation. A resurrecting God loves to surprise and unbalance. Critics said nasty things about Jesus; nobody ever accused him of being dull.

CERTITUDE

Unassailable, uncontested conviction that, on your own, you have the means of knowing what's what. In the New Testament, the Greek word for certainty, asphaleia, *comes from the same root as our word "asphalt." What does that tell you?*

Though a quest beloved by the modern world, when it comes to most of the really important things in life, certainty is a fiction. Sorry, European Enlightenment; in our modern lust for sure facts, knockdown arguments, and unassailable proof, our world didn't expand; it shrank. Modernity deceived us into thinking that we, by stepping back and dispassionately applying the right epistemological method, could understand everything. Christians, on the other hand, believe that mystery is best understood by falling in love with it, allowing ourselves to be embraced by the inexplicable, understanding everything with the help of what we don't understand. Jesus is a reality no more uncertain than your conviction that your mother adores you or that the one who sleeps beside you is your beloved. People sometimes complain that we know too little about Jesus to bet our

21

lives on him. Truth to tell, we are evasive and self-deceitful, so there's a sense in which we know more about self-revealing Jesus than we know about us.

Some apologists argue that if you found a watch lying on the sidewalk, you would ascertain that the complex creation had a creator. A wonderful world presupposes the certain existence of a divine world maker.

Trouble is, scripture nowhere claims that God made a beautifully complex world and then tossed it aside. Creation names the loving, constant interaction between God and the material. God keeps making something out of what is not much of anything. Creation is inherently, continuously, relentlessly relational and is better understood through relationship than explanation.

Because God is the One who turns toward us, determined to be in relationship, we don't get to make up our minds about God. Christ won't allow us to step back from either God or the world and presume to be objective observers, tourists just passing through, disinterestedly deciding for ourselves just what is and is not there.

It's strange that Christians should be accused of being narrow-minded and simplistic when belief in and relationship with God requires a willingness to be wrong, to start over and revise, and now and then to have your mind blown by a God whose love for you is too great and grand to be fully comprehended. Confusion, befuddlement, and wonder come with the job.

Still, by the grace of God, the mystery of Christianity is ascertainable. God enjoys giving us all we need to believe. Doubting Thomas was given bodily, tangible proof that the one who appeared to him on Easter evening was indeed Jesus. To those who asked, "Are you the messiah or should we seek another?" Jesus offered visible evidence: the blind see, the deaf hear, the crippled walk, the dead are raised, and the poor have good news preached to them.

When the world demands, "Prove that God is who you claim God to be," we don't trot out our apologetic arguments, attempting to present the Christian faith as if it weren't weird. All we've got to show as validation of our God is our lives, evidence of what a relational God can do. Besides, any god who can be proved by us is too little a god to be our God.

If ever you come across a knock-down, irresistible argument for God, or absolute, certain truth, your life will be easier if you worship that rather than Jesus.

Let's thank God that Jesus asks for our love rather than our understanding.

CHILD

The kingdom of God has a small door; grownups must stoop to enter.

Whenever a child shows up in a sermon, it's a warning that the preacher is about to do a deep dive into twaddle and blather. Hearing Jesus say, "Let the little children come to me, don't hinder them," sounds sweet because our culture sentimentalizes children even as abortions run a million a year and there's widespread child abuse and neglect. We treat our youngest as we treat our eldest: warehousing, institutionalizing them. Our grown-up productivity and upward mobility can't be limited by dependents.

In Jesus's day, children were of value mostly as the Near Eastern equivalent to our Social Security. Childlessness meant a grim old age. While allegedly a gift of God, children are generally depicted in scripture as weak, ignorant, and disobedient. "When I was a child, I used to speak like a child, reason like a child, think like a child," says Paul, "But now that I have become a man, I've put an end to childish things." Not a great endorsement of childhood.

Which makes all the more striking that when the disciples complained, "Lord, we can't pay attention to your theology lecture because of these rambunctious children. Send them to the church nursery." Jesus responded, "Let the little children come to me. Don't hinder them. They know more about God than you grownups." And he took a child and put an immature, unruly, difficult to manage, impudent child in the middle of them to help them pay attention.

"Let the children come to me," could well be the most radical, countercultural statement Jesus uttered, much like what he said about the poor and the outcast, only more so.

You never become so independent and competent that you are too old to "turn your lives around and become like this little child." When, in spite of your years, you revert, are out of control, ignorant, empty, lost, unruly, dependent, disobedient, that's a good time to remember Jesus saying, "Don't hold the little ones back. Let 'em come to me. This, my kingdom."

CHRISTIAN

Not a favorite designation for followers of Jesus in the New Testament.

Acts calls us simply followers of the Way. To be with Jesus is to be on the Way. Maybe that's why all the Gospels portray Jesus and his followers as on a perpetual road trip. A Christian is someone on the way with Jesus in a journey that's more interesting than if Christ had allowed you to stay home. As with any journey, you're not sure of what you're getting into when you stumble after Jesus. You don't know the exact destination or what hazards lie ahead. All you know is that you are on the road with Jesus, headed in the right direction.

After a church fight over whether or not the good news of Jesus ought to be shared even with pagans, and the early church stopped dithering over the question, "Who ought we exclude?," and began to plot, "Who can we invite?" Only then were the followers of the Way called Christians.

That ought to tell us something.

CHRISTOLOGY

Christianity is about Christ, God turned toward us. Whenever the world says, "Tell us something we don't know," or "Got hope?" or even, "Take a political stand," the church gives witness, "Jesus Christ."

John says that nobody has ever seen God. That held true until we saw Jesus, the whole truth about God, as much of God as we ever hope to see in this world, God up close and personal, God condescending, turning to us.

Jesus keeps us from making "God" mean anything we please. He not only turns to us and becomes one of us, but he also stands against us, contends with us, woos, wrestles, welcomes us back to God. In every age Jesus always breaks free of our attempts to tame him. How he loves to surprise.

Little is gained by trying to separate the so-called historical Jesus from the alleged Christ of faith, dividing Christ's divinity from his humanity. In him, the divine thoroughly assumes the human; the human is utterly embraced by the divine. Then human/divine Christ calls disciples who show the world how to live in human history now that God is with us.

Though Jesus is God showing up in our history, the resurrection-ascension thrusts Jesus out beyond the clutches of history. In spite of Jesus's impressive ministry in Judea, what he does in your town right now is even more remarkable.

The New Testament is the only source of reliable information about Jesus. While there's lots we don't know about Jesus, what we don't know is unimportant for our salvation. With Jesus, we've always known more than we've been able to process.

Jesus was crucified as a vain attempt to shut him up. Yet in every human culture, in all times and places, Christ has risen up and spoken for himself. He will get his way and have his say. Nobody has ever created a culture so hostile, an intellectual defense so solid, a political system so godless, clergy so corrupt, a sermon so narcotic that it keeps Jesus from speaking up and speaking out when he wants. From the first, Jesus went where he was not sought and showed up to people who didn't ask to meet him.

God, the brown-skinned Jew from Nazareth who was born unexpectedly, preached sermons that were sometimes well received, but mostly not, embraced the untouchable and paid for it dearly, lived briefly, died violently, rose unexpectedly and returned to the same friends who disappointed him.

Thank God.

CHURCH

Ecclesia, called out. Body of Christ. Everybody and anybody Christ drags in the door.

In the Apostle's Creed, when we "believe in the church," we are saying that we believe in the peculiar way that the resurrected Christ takes up room in the world. As Christ's visible, vocal presence, if people meet Jesus, the usual route is through his church—which has always made uneasy those who know the sorry state of your average church.

He did not come to disembodied angels, he came to us, says the Letter to the Hebrews. That's why the church loves the parable of the dragnet that indiscriminately hauls in sea creatures, clean and unclean, and Jesus's story of the good wheat and the bad weeds growing together. Who in the congregation is valuable "wheat," and who's worthless "weeds?" Jesus isn't telling. You'll have to wait. The sorting's not up to us. For now, you are stuck worshipping Jesus with people who are not your type.

We know the center of the circle that is the kingdom of God—Christ—but not its circumference. It's like a man who sent out invitations to a party. Nobody came. In anger the Lord of the banquet invited the folk who had nowhere to go and could appreciate a free meal, in short, folk with whom we wouldn't be caught dead on a Saturday night. That's the kingdom of God, the church its first installment.

Most really nasty church fights are collateral damage from Jesus's absurdly broad delineation of the kingdom of Heaven, his insistence on saving those with whom I have little in common. Nobody withdraws from a congregation saying, "Jesus demands too much." They leave muttering, "Love Jesus; can't stand his friends."

That's why the New Testament loves the reciprocal pronoun "one another" (*allēlōn*): live in harmony with one another, admonish one another, wait for one another, build up one another, submit to one another, forgive one another, pray for one another, and that which congregations find most difficult, put up with one another.

In church, Christ keeps reminding us of what a gift each can be, insisting that we call these oddballs "brother," "sister," and that we allow ourselves to be called the same by them. Church gives us something good to do with our gifts. Christian truth is a group product, not a discovery of the solitary individual. In church we learn dependency upon others (some of them dead for a thousand years) who help us to endure the rigors of discipleship.

After hammering one of his most divided, forlorn congregations, Paul concludes with, "You are the body of Christ." Us? The church, for better or worse, yes, even the U.M.C. Inc., is Christ's visible, bodily appeal to the world. Jesus could have written a book, established an efficient system of public welfare, or founded an ethical improvement colloquium. Instead, gathering ordinary people with a reckless, "Follow me!" he invited them to his revolution.

Many of us found, during the isolation of the pandemic, that watching virtual church—alone—is less than the real thing. Still, it's easier to love Jesus than his physique. "Spirituality" is all the rage—

feeling religious, sort of—church without the bother of people who fail to be as vaguely, innocuously spiritual as you. "Spirituality"— Jesus on the cheap, without a bride or a body, Jesus stripped of you and me.

Sometimes the bride of Christ sleeps around. Church becomes our last stand against God, church morphed into a civic club with a sacred tint, a safe haven in which to cower as you lick your wounds, a cafeteria where starving people are handed a menu to chew on rather than invited to a banquet, a firecracker rather than a stick of dynamite, wine turned into water at the Sunday Service.

Still, church is Christ's great strategy for getting what God wants. We are saved together—including the aging soprano who, if the preacher had guts, should be retired from the choir, and the right-wing bigot who just happens to be the congregation's most generous donor, and the brat who keeps kicking the back of my pew—or saved not at all. It's a heck of a way to inaugurate the kingdom of heaven, but it appears to be God's way.

Though Christ calls us to a 10k marathon, most congregations are couch potatoes. Christ's body is crucified, full of holes, with a nasty gash in the side. Yet, for all of its wounds, church is the way God shows up, God's great plan for the redemption of creation. Whatever Jesus wants to do, from the first, he chooses to do it not alone, promising, "If just two or three show up for the Wednesday evening Bible study, count me in."

"Look at you," Paul tells one of his congregations. "Not the brightest candles in the box, not many mighty, no celebrities." Then the great mystery: "God chose what the world considers weak to shame the strong. And God chose what the world considers low-class and low-life—what is considered to be nothing—to reduce what is considered to be something to nothing." We foolish, weak, low-class, low-lifes, we happy few, shamers of the strong. Church.

The Revelation says that there will be no temple in the New Jerusalem. Maybe that's because we won't need the poor old church to keep us on the way; we will have arrived. The God who occasionally drops in for the Sunday service will dwell with us forever. Until then, the best God has given is church.

CLERGY

The leaders selected for religious duties in the church, variously known as pastor, minister, deacon, elder, reverend, and bishop.

From the first, leadership is not optional for followers of Christ. The mission Christ gives is too difficult to wait until we feel like it. So, drawing from the ranks of the baptized, the church invented clergy. In spite of fancy vestments, arcane language, and ceremonial claptrap, clergy have mainly functional rather than sacerdotal significance. They are Christ's means of keeping his body in motion.

Clerical sin by demagogic, unaccountable, big-headed clergy has been church at its worst. However, clergy dominance of the church is usually not due to a power grab by priests. Down through the ages the laity have been all too willing to dump their baptismally assigned ministry upon surrogate clergy. All the baptized have responsibility to witness, serve, give, and to speak truth. As far as God is concerned, everybody in Israel or the church, even without an MDiv from an accredited seminary, is a priest. An overworked pastor is always a cleric with an inadequate theology of baptism.

Yet somebody has to convene, orchestrate, organize, be blamed for congregational gaffes, teach and tell the truth in order to equip the saints (all the baptized) for the work of ministry. Thus the church regularly lays hands upon the heads of regular Christians making them pastors, priests, deacons, elders, bishops.

People are not made clergy because of their superior intelligence, high morality, or spiritual acumen—a close look at your pastor will disabuse you of that fallacy. Clergy's sole sanction is the behest of God and the church.

By whatever names the church calls its clergy, however the church organizes itself—including how the church vets, chooses, holds accountable, and authorizes its leaders—is a matter of taste and tradition rather than biblical warrant. A few, utterly human, vocationally reckless, called by God and the church from the ranks of the faithful, say, "Okay, okay, Lord. I give in. I hope you know what you are doing. In spite of my self-doubts, I'll take responsibility for helping the church stay the church."

Clergy: one of Christ's sly stratagems for getting what he wants from his church.

CONSCIENCE

Knowing right from wrong without knowing Christ.

The philosopher Immanuel Kant was greatly impressed with the "moral law within." Christians are not. Moral discernment comes not from within us; it's what's happened to us.

Be careful of listening too attentively to your "still, small voice." What you hear may be no more than the way you were brought up. To "just let your conscience be your guide" is to risk stumbling after a fool. Your conscience may be clear because your head is empty.

Jesus counters the unreliability of your conscience by breathing upon us his Holy Spirit, thus stoking, funding, fueling our moral imaginations, writing God's law upon our self-deceitful hearts, giving us guidance better than we were born with. Says Paul, "I no longer live, but Christ lives in me."

CONVERSION

Detoxification. The God whom we wanted on our terms, taking us on God's terms.

Crabby Tertullian said, "Christians are made, not born." Christians come from the church's baptismal font, not people's loins. Because Jesus and his kingdom fundamentally challenge everything we thought we knew for sure, conversion is part of the project. Paul didn't know whether to describe what happened to him, when he met Christ, as birth or death. It felt like both at the same time.

Christian is not synonymous with being born American. Conversion is mandatory. Rarely is the Christian life an orderly progression toward God. More typically, it's a series of jerks and jolts, lurches to the left or right. Fasten your seat belts, you could end up miles from here.

Nobody ever gets so adept at being a Christian that you lose your amateur status. Seldom a one-and-done experience, as Christ told old Nicodemus, "You must be born again," to which Wesleyans add, and again, and again, and probably again. Birth to death, darkness to light then, at the end, death leading to life.

Warning: I'm not saying that the Holy Spirit takes advantage of us when we're down, but if you are going through a particularly painful time in your life, know that Christ enjoys showing up at such moments and working them to his gain. On the other hand, if you are happy with the life you are living, pleased as punch with the person you are, happy with the world as it is, be careful hanging around Jesus. He may take you just as you are but never leaves you there. Everyone he touches, Christ transforms.

Extreme makeover, like our salvation, is something that God does to you rather than something you do for yourself. Baptism is not a declaration that you've at last found a faith that works for you but rather your bodacious willingness to let this faith work on you.

Christ's baptismal promises: you are not doomed to plod along in the life your parents handed you. By the power of the Holy Spirit, anybody can be a saint, everyone can have fate transformed into destiny by God. You, even you, can hit the road with Jesus. "Come die with me," he says, "that you might rise to the life I wanted to give you in the first place."

As Jesus headed down the road one day a man comes up and asks him a deep theological question: "What must I do to inherit eternal life?" One Gospel says that the man was a "ruler," another that he was "young." All agree that he was rich. Jesus brushes him off by telling him to obey all the commandments. Turns out this man is really good at being good; he's been totally obedient since he was a kid, a hard-core success, both materially and spiritually. Then Jesus speaks those converting words that Christians like me have always wished he hadn't: "Go . . . sell . . . give . . . follow me."

If you journey with Jesus, expect a rough ride.

COVENANT

Promise.

Once God said, "I will be your God and you will be my people"—without asking our approval, pledging to love us even though time and again we didn't know how to love in return—God forever cast God's lot with us. Though we have given the Lord ample opportunity to regret getting mixed up with sinners like us, God has shown faithful, dogged determination to have a family, in spite of our repeated infidelity.

Toward the beginning, there were moments. The first human progeny committed the first fratricide as Cain bashed in the head of his brother. Once humanity got a taste of blood, head-bashing and sibling-despising run rampant. God saw that God's intentions for humanity had gone awry and that "the inclination of their hearts was only evil all the time." Repenting of ever having gotten mixed up in the human project, God throws creation in reverse.

In a terrible forty-day flood, the earth was allowed to revert to its formless watery chaos. Only one family survived along with pairs of all the animals on the ark. When finally the waters subsided, the first thing God did was to make a promise to Noah: "I'm establishing my covenant with you and all your descendants. Never again will I give up on my creation." God's powerful bow was hung in the clouds, as "a sign of the covenant between me and the earth." A rainbow. If ever again humanity screws up (spoiler alert, we will), God will glance at the bow in the clouds, remember the covenant, and not give us what we deserve.

Lord, keep your eye on that rainbow.

Those who talk of God's "unconditional love" haven't got it quite right. God loves us as we are but never leaves us that way. (Lovers are notorious for setting high expectations for their beloved.) In covenant, God first says what God will do for us. Then God tells us what God expects of us. Better than unconditional, God's love is vocational.

When we are lost and wandering, or when we feel no responsibility for anyone but ourselves and our families, it can be either reassuring or annoying to let the rainbow remind us that God has covenanted to be our God *and* for us to be God's. It's a comfort to know that our relationship with God, our discipleship, was God's idea before it was ours.

CREATION

What God does for a living.

The Bible begins, "In the beginning . . . God said, 'Let there be light!'" It's encouraging to know that God likes to start things, to create something out of nothing. (After all, look at you.) It's heartening that God loves to talk. (It's not your job either to initiate or to sustain the divine/human conversation.) No matter the mess we make of the world, it's bolstering to believe that God thought of it, and when done, stepped back from creation and marveled, "That's good, real good."

No sooner had God created us than God said to the humans, "Hey, I've enjoyed creating; now you try it. Be fruitful, multiply!" (One of God's most enjoyable commands to obey.)

Throughout our history with God, everything begins with, "And God said . . ." No newness, no something out of nothing, no "good" unless the creator keeps creating. God never stops being the innovative, resourceful, enthusiastic conversationalist. Therein, our first, last, best hope for never being bored.

We are the "image" (Greek: *ikon*) "of God." In biblical times, a conquering monarch set up an image of himself in the city he had subjugated, just to let people know who was in charge. If we are God's images, then maybe God cares for the world through us stewards, God's ambassadors in God's world. Noah survived the most dramatic instance of climate change in scripture by being enlisted by God to save God's beloved creatures. Are we being enlisted for similar creation care?

Trouble is, think much about the climate crisis and you are driven to despair. Too little too late. Yet remembering that the "earth is the Lord's," we take heart. In believing that "God so loved the world," the main thing Christians have to contribute to the environmental movement is hope. Though the whole creation groans as we await redemption, Christians not only wait but work in hope knowing that God keeps loving God's world and has given us a part to play in creation's care.

Calling it creation rather than merely nature is acknowledgement that nothing is self-produced or free standing and autonomous. God continues to create, refuses to leave good enough alone, and loves to make things. "It is God who hath made us, not we ourselves" a most un-American thought you might overlook because it's in a song.

You and the cosmos have got God's fingerprints all over you.

CREED

"I believe." What you say after you get the news that God is for you.

Over the years, the church has found that a good way to keep in conversation with God is to put the core of our believing into creeds. A creed like the Apostles' Creed keeps beckoning you back to the basic stuff of the faith, should you be tempted either to be too timid or too imaginative in your believing. Creeds say what we believe or are on our way to believing.

Creeds tether us to our forebears in the faith, reminding us that we don't have to make up our believing as we go. Notable for their brevity, creeds keep the Christian faith simple, straightforward, and tied to what God in Christ has actually done in human time.

When someone says, "If you are going to be a Christian you must believe that . . ." —if it ain't in the creed, you can say, "Thanks, but I've got enough on my plate already."

If you have difficulty believing some tenet of the creed, you need not cross your fingers. It's a statement of the church's belief, not a personal declaration of how much doctrine you can swallow without choking. Just keep saying it, affirming the creeds the same way you sing the church's hymns. Belief will come to you. And if it doesn't, the church promises to keep on believing for you until you get there.

CROSS

One of the most vicious, publicly humiliating forms of capital punishment ever devised. Excruciating.

Jesus didn't die peacefully in his sleep; he was agonizingly tortured to death, receiving nonviolently the world's violence. Crucifixion is Roman public murder that's disturbingly analogous to American lynching.

"He came unto his own and his own received him not." He offered us open-handed fellowship. Our collective response? "Crucify him!"

The cross is a mirror that reflects who we really are as well as a window where we are given a privileged look into the heart of who God is. Who are we? Those who viciously rejected God. Who is God? The one who raised crucified, despised, betrayed Jesus from the dead, the one who decisively, graciously rejected our violent refusal.

A crucified messiah? The thought that God's anointed would suffer and die as a common criminal was unthinkable. "God forbid this should happen to you," said Peter, the premier disciple. While we were still trying to get our heads around the oxymoron of God pushed out of the world on a cross, Jesus predicted not only that he would go to the cross but we would as well. God forbid this should happen to us.

The cross proves that God is more than a projection of our desires. As Paul said in Romans, we might be willing to die for a really good person, but Christ shows that he is unlike us by dying for sinners like us.

"All who want to come after me must say no to themselves, take up their cross, and follow me. All who want to save their lives will lose them. But all who lose their lives because of me and because of the good news will save them." Because no congregation has ever tried to nail me to a cross or throw me over a cliff postsermon, I've got some explaining to do.

The cross is not a bad back or a difficult-to-get-along-with relative. The "cross" is the predictable suffering, rejection, and maybe even death that comes our way because we are attempting to walk Jesus's way, a way that is counter to the world's way.

So the question is not "Why did Jesus have to suffer for us?" but "Why must we suffer because of Jesus?" Why does Jesus allow people to beat up on his best friends, sometimes as badly as they beat up on him?

Yet when we've done our worst—put to death God's only Son—God turns our sin into the means of our salvation. Remember that, next time you either do or receive the worst.

DEATH

End of life.

All that lives, dies. Like grass, we thrive in the morning; by evening we fade. When we die, we die, returning to the dust from which we came. Tears and wailing are appropriate when the sting of death separates us from our beloved. Of all human enemies, death is the ultimate. Thus Jesus wept for his deceased friend and in Gethsemane, Jesus prayed, "I don't want to die."

God gives life, but doesn't tell us for how long. Upfront, God promises to kill us all. Every day of life is a step nearer death. Death is not an injustice; it's the God-given limit for creatures who, for all our potential and possibility, must die. No wonder fears of death—

along with vain human attempts to deceive ourselves about death's inevitability—consume us. Get a face lift, smear on rouge, work out at the gym, endow a chair at the university, chisel your name in granite—this too, shall pass.

Behold, you'll never retrieve the time you lost reading the previous paragraph.

A Stoic stiff upper lip, Platonic claims of some immortal soul, are no match for the Grim Reaper, nor are sentimental bromides like, "She'll live on in our memories," or "He's gone to a better place."

All the more amazing that Christians believe that death isn't the worst that can happen to us. The martyrs thought it better to be killed than to give a pinch of incense on Caesar's altar. Sadder than dying is never to have lived. When you are baptized, you die, says Paul. "He died that we might die to sin." Baptism is drowning that leads to life, dress rehearsal for the day of our dying, teaching us day-by-day to let go that to which we tightly though futilely cling. Want to be a better Christian? All you must do is die. Christians are those who are being trained how to die too soon.

It's Christ's resurrection that enables Christians not to be dominated by fear of dying, to be honest about death and therefore despise death, and yet be hopeful for life after this life. The same God who raised Jesus somehow reaches in, defeats our enemy death, and takes us along as well, making good on his promise, "Because I live, you live too."

Seen through the lens of the resurrection, death ceases to be a curse, a thief, the final enemy and begins to appear as forgiveness, blessing, sometimes even friend. We are surprised that as the door closes on life, God unlocks a gate that we cannot open for ourselves, Christ going head-to-head with death—our physical death in the future, our captivity to death in the present—defeating death.

"We do not grieve as those who have no hope." Grief, tears, anguish are normal, natural, predictable responses to death. Yet even in the face of death, we have hope not in human immortality or invincibility but in the truth of Christ's promise, "Because I live, you will too!"

DECALOGUE

Ten words, only ten, when God could have commanded so much more.

Moses is told to stand up to Pharaoh and say, "Let my people go!"

Why? Because God is against enslavement? God is a liberationist? God doesn't like sharing God's chosen with Pharaoh? Yes, but all Moses is given to say is, "Let my people go that they may worship me in the wilderness."

Stiff-necked Pharaoh scoffs, "I'll send one of my court chaplains to the ghetto, and you can sing some of those spirituals that you folks do so well. Just be damn sure you are back at work on Monday."

Negotiations follow, refusals, a series of plagues, all culminating in Pharaoh's finally saying, "Get the hell out of Egypt and never come back."

At last the Hebrews are free in the wilderness. But it has been so long since they have worshipped the true and living God, they have forgotten how.

Moses says, "I'll go up Mount Sinai and get the right liturgical rubrics from the Lord."

"Are you into high church smells and bells, or do you prefer tacky guitars and praise songs?" asks Moses.

Yahweh responds, "Write this down. Don't kill. Don't steal. Don't have sex with other people's spouses. Envy not what I've given others. Don't consort with other gods; I created you, own you, have plans for you."

Moses says, "This doesn't sound like any liturgy I've been part of."

"That's where I'm different from other gods," says Yahweh. "You worship me by living like you belong to me. In Israel, there's no boundary between worship and ethics. Your genitalia, cuisine, asses, money, marriages—mine!"

In this newly liberated family, everybody's free to be a priest, all saints utilized in achieving God's worship in the world, just like God used Moses and all of Israel.

Ten words point the way.

DISCIPLESHIP

Following Jesus. Ambassadors for Christ.

In turning to us, God demonstrates God's choice to work not alone. Christ, the great delegator. Jesus didn't ask the intellectual, "Does my teaching make sense?" He commanded the vocational: "Follow me."

The God who mugged church enemy number one, Saul-Soon-to-Become-Paul, is the God who refuses to stay dead and delights in working up the unlikeliest into a "chosen vessel" to bear "my name before the Gentiles, and kings, and the children of Israel." If God chose a person like Saul, God could choose anybody.

Discipleship is the way Christ rescues you from vain attempts to make something of your life. God gives you a job that's more important than you. Faced with a broken world, creation out of kilter, God doesn't "send in the Marines." God casts forth the meek, foolish, and weak. Us.

Having called the Twelve (with mixed results) Jesus sends out Seventy-Two, two-by-two (his work, too dangerous to do solo). They return (with joy) amazed that, "It works! Even the demons obey us, though we've had inadequate theological training." Jesus replies, "I saw Satan fall from heaven like lightning!"

Even with our many limitations, we are Christ's major means of dethroning Satan. We are God's way of turning the world upside down so God can put things right side up.

DOUBT

Intellectual reservations about Christ. Typical reaction to the truth. Often a symptom of an exaggerated confidence in our own capacity to render a verdict on Jesus. Proof that it's impossible to believe in Christ unaided by the Holy Spirit.

Doubt is not necessarily the opposite of faith; sometimes doubt is faith's antecedent. Any God who can't be humanly doubted can never be your God.

Whenever somebody says of Christ, "I don't believe," it's important for you to add, "yet." Because of an active, resourceful Christ, there is good reason to doubt your doubts; Christ gives you freedom to doubt, but not to have the last word.

ELECTION

God's choice.

Once God promised, "I will be your God and you will be my people," the direction was cast for human history. First God elects Israel, not because of any positive quality in Israel but simply because "God loves you." Chosen not for privilege, Israel is given a task—to be a light shining forth to all nations, a showcase of what God can do once God elects a people.

God's universality is accomplished through particularity. In the story of election, God starts small—Abraham and Sarah—expands to a people, Israel, then contracts into a Jew from Nazareth, enlarges to twelve disciples, then seventy, exploding into Jerusalem, Judea, Samaria, and the ends of the earth. A few chosen for the universal good of all.

"I'm going to take back my beloved but wayward creation," says the electing God. "Guess who's going to help me?"

If you've been led to believe that God is a cosmic bureaucrat, just following the rules, treating everyone the same, think again. God gets things done by playing favorites, giving them not privilege but rather responsibility. As God told Abraham and Sarah, through their family, "all the families of the earth will be blessed."

"God chose what is foolish in the world." Why? "To shame the wise, to mock the strong." Even though we elected Barabbas when asked for an up or down vote on Jesus's execution, Jesus elected us.

God's particularity is scandalously inscrutable. "How odd of God to choose the Jews." Why is Able chosen over Cain? Why Jacob rather than Esau? Why Israel instead of Egypt? Most inscrutable of all: Why you?

Knowing that we have been elected by God to be with God and to work for God—not because of who we are or what we have done but because of who God is and what God in Jesus Christ is doing—is great freedom. As Jesus told his bumbling disciples, "You didn't choose me, but I chose you." So when someone says, "You are a sorry excuse for a Christian," you can retort, "Take it up with the Lord! My discipleship was Jesus's idea of a good time before it was mine. You think I would have chosen this path if Christ had left the choosing up to me?"

EMIGRANT

Someone who leaves home to begin a new life elsewhere.

As Israel said, "My forebear was a wandering Aramean," so Christians know that we are exiles, sojourners, and immigrants ("resident aliens" NRSV). The first thing the Holy Family did after Jesus's birth was to immigrate to Egypt, seeking sanctuary. There's no way to enter the Christian faith except as an emigrant displaced from one kingdom to another. Naturalized citizens, strangers and immigrants, all, we sojourners must never forget, "You know what it's like to be an immigrant, because you were immigrants in the land of Egypt."

Paul says it's crucially important not to bed down here. Peripatetic Christ renders his followers homeless. This world, for all its grandeur, is not our home. Maybe that's why the Holy Spirit has never been impressed by national borders. Something in Jesus doesn't love a wall.

ESCHATOLOGY

Talk of last things.

"The end," as both human history's termination and its purpose. Good news if this world has given you hell, bad news if you think this is as good as it gets.

Paul characterized his preaching as a first installment on the eschatological, old-age ending, new-age beginning yes of God. The church exists to sign, to signal, and to be a sneak preview of the endings and beginnings God means to make among us. Surprise. God isn't impressed by the world we have made.

Eschatological thinking enables us to combine honesty about the sorry state of the present with hope in the future, hope not based upon naive fantasies of human potential but grounded in what we know from stories of God's agency in the past and present. The future is unveiled to us so that we might live God's future right now.

What does tomorrow look like? God only knows. Of this we are sure: because the future is what God makes of it, there'll be surprises.

ETERNAL LIFE

Nothing about us—progeny, endowed chairs, mutual funds—lasts. Only God has a future.

"I wish this moment could last forever." It doesn't. Yet in that moment maybe God gives you just a taste of eternity. Eternity doesn't mean time going on forever, infinity. It means being with God who, though entering time in the incarnation, is beyond time.

In those delicious, glorious moments—sometimes experienced in worship in church, sometimes holding the hand of your beloved beside a lake in the moonlight— time stands still, or races forward, or melts away, and you are brought close to something beyond or above or beneath ever fleeting time. "For this I was made," we exclaim.

Because of the work of Jesus Christ, what you've experienced only briefly, in fits and starts, shall one day be always.

Jesus's friend Lazarus is dying. "Come quick! Lazarus whom you love is sick!"

After a three-day delay(!), Jesus shows up at the cemetery and tells Lazarus's sisters Mary and Martha, that their brother shall live. Martha says something like, "Yeah, I know that one day, someday, there will be something called the resurrection." Jesus then tells her, "I'm resurrection. I'm life." Whenever Jesus turns toward the dead, eternal life is now, be they buried in a cemetery or in a boring life.

To believe that Jesus is eternal life is to have a hope that in life, in death, in any promised life beyond death, the God who owes us nothing promises to give us everything: not merely an extension of life as we know it, but rather life as God wants it. Christ, who in this life showed that he would go to any lengths to have us, would have us for all eternity.

ETHICS

Who we are; the science of human virtues and vices.

What we should do, ought not do, and don't do: living in accord with reality (otherwise known as the Trinity). An account of us at our courageous best and at our self-deceitful worst. "Ethics" doesn't mean much without the modifier "Christian."

Christian ethics not only attempt to answer big questions like, "How ought I to live?" but also bigger ones like, "Whom do I adore?" as well as, "Who is Jesus enabling me to be?" Not simply the dilemma, "What ought I to do?" but also, "What is God doing in the world and how can I jump on board?" Generally speaking, the substance of a supposedly Christian ethical position is revealed by how often the proponent refers vaguely to "God" or "the quality of human life" and how little Jesus is mentioned.

In commending Christian ethics the church doesn't claim that your life will be made less stressful or that you'll feel better about yourself; just the opposite could be the case. (Look where living a godly life got Jesus and his first disciples.) The claim is that the one who told us to forgive our enemies, give to the poor, keep the promises of marriage, and live nonviolently in a world at war just happened to be the Son of God.

By calling us, God enlisted our cooperation and participation, but—thank God—the fate of God's world has not been left up to us. Generally speaking, Christians don't behave as we do in order to get somewhere with God. We act as those who've arrived. God has turned to us, so we gratefully want to live in a way that turns us toward God.

The more we obey Christ, the closer we find ourselves drawn to Christ, the more frequently we find ourselves falling flat on our faces. Nobody should attempt to live and act like a Christian who doesn't know the Christ who forgives sinners.

God loves us enough not to allow us to stumble along and find our way to God on our own. All Christian ethics is social ethics, life dependent upon friends who tell us truth we don't want to hear, whose moral lapses force us to summon the courage to speak truth to them, and who then sustain us when we fail to live up to Jesus's expectations of us.

God gives rules, principles, laws, patterns, exemplars, but most of all God gives Jesus. Nobody is expected to be ethical on their own, and, after Jesus, we've never been on our own. Christianity is not first of all about being good. The logic is this: because we now know that God is good, how then should we live? What others call "ethics" or "morals" is for Christians a form of worship, living in an accountable relationship with Jesus Christ.

You'll know that the Holy Spirit has indeed done its work in you when you do right without thinking about it, when righteousness is second nature. You're not trying hard to be faithful; faithful is who, by God's grace, you have become.

Sometimes it's best to leap before you look. Thoughtful ethical deliberation can be our sly attempt to avoid—rather than to obey—the crucified Christ. "How can I do the right thing without detriment, pain, or difficulty?" Answer: you can't.

Maybe if all of us who love Christ lived more like Christ the world would be a better place. The world might be better but, remembering the cost Christ paid for his ethics, the world could be more dangerous for Christians.

EUCHARIST

A meal that means everything that a meal means—when Jesus invites us to his table.

In a faith full of words, it's delightful that Jesus the preacher comes to the summit of his ministry, the depths of his deep love, and says simply, "Have some bread. Take some wine. My body, my blood, given for you."

He who was among us in Palestine now becomes present to us in bread and wine. How often should we receive the Lord's Supper? Only as often as we need to be close to God. Who is most worthy to receive the blessed bread and wine? Those who are honest to God empty.

Every time we receive Christ in bread and wine, we go through the motions of embracing the materiality that is at the heart of the mystery of being Christian. We come forward to the table, hold out hungry, open hands, needing a gift we can't earn. Then having been as much in the presence of Christ as we shall be on this earth, fed, strengthened, and nourished, we can go on.

EVANGELISM

Sharing the good news—"Hey, you're included"—making all the more strange that many "evangelicals" are known for their lists of who ought to be excluded.

When you love someone, you quite naturally want others to love them with you. Good news begs to be shared. Evangelism gives news to those who don't know whereby they will know that in Jesus Christ God knows them. If you see something wonderful, you'll point it out to others so that they can enjoy the wonder too. Evangelists simply say, "Come and see."

47

The world is right to judge the good news by the lives it produces. Sadly, "good news" is the last thing many people think when they hear "church." Evangelism is not only telling but also showing, being the church and living our lives in such a way that it provokes others to exclaim, "Look at them love!"

Paul says that you are Christ's letter written to the world, God's appeal to all: "Be reconciled!" You, God's lights amid the gloom: shine!

That some haven't heard and others reject, doesn't mean that the news is untrue. More probably it means that we have done a lousy job of broadcasting.

In a day when evangelism sometimes reduces the gospel to what fits on a bumper sticker, it's remarkable that when the church was fighting for its life, early Christian preachers like Paul didn't shrink good news to otherwise widely available common sense. Rather, they carefully articulated distinctions between Christ and empire. If the empire's functionaries pushed back against the politics of the gospel (i.e., Jesus is Lord, Caesar is not), Paul didn't retreat, reducing the public truth of Christ to something safely personal and private (such as, I believe that Jesus is Lord, but that's just my personal opinion).

Is it arrogant to witness to others in the hope that God may convert them? It's more arrogant to keep good news to ourselves, as if it's our possession rather than God's gift and our responsibility. Why cower before the world's lies into which people have been converted (God is absent, what's dead stays that way, though Jesus is not Lord, you might become a lord unto yourself if you try real hard, etc.)? Let's go head-to-head with the world, allow Jesus to roam freely, and see who's still standing by the end of the argument.

In leaning over to speak to the world, sometimes we fall in. "What do you think you really must have in order to make your life worth living?" we ask potential converts, promising, "Jesus can deliver." Luring folks to Jesus by promising them what Jesus has no intention of giving isn't evangelism; it's false advertising.

In a society of vast loneliness, it's tempting for church to say, "Come, we'll give you community. Friendliest church in town." This ploy overlooks how "community" can be an excuse for avoiding conflict, huddling with those who look a lot like you, hiding from God in the safety of the herd. Evangelism isn't an appeal to people's self-centeredness that then baits-and-switches them into relationship with the selfless one who said, "Take up your cross and follow."

"Our church's main concern is _____" (fill in the blank with whatever you value more than the church), is often a signal that a congregation has tired of the rigors of worshipping God and is now kowtowing to whatever people find more engaging than the Trinity.

A pastor fatigued by a cloying congregation is usually a symptom of evangelism gone bad. Rather than help Christ gather and then deploy his people, a cluster of selfish, demanding consumers have huddled because through wrong-headed evangelistic appeals they're misled into thinking that church is about them.

Evangelism begins in the heart of God, in God's determination to have a people. Thus Paul speaks of the "gospel of God" or "God's good news." Evangelism is what God does, a name for God's constant activity among us, God flooding the world with truth. Anywhere we evangelists go, Christ got there first. We announce and share the gospel, but only God can verify.

God's most tender question, spoken at the first: "Where are you?" Jesus's rebuke to those who accused him of being too evangelistic: I've "come to seek and save the lost."

EXODUS

Leading out, liberation, God taking back what other gods purloined from God.

Jesus is the new Moses continuing the exodus from slavery to freedom. No wonder that Black congregations—caught in the web of White racism—love to recount the exodus, whereas many white American congregations—benefiting from and feeling more at home in the American empire—get jittery when either Moses (or Jesus) commands, "Let my people go!"

Something is gained in any exodus from Egypt to the Promised Land, but something is lost as well. The loss may be painful. Freedom can be frightening. Even though God may be leading us out, sometimes it's hard to let go of the life we once knew in order to venture God knows where. In Egypt, at least we had three meals a day.

Still, God created no one for enslavement to Egypt, white supremacy, heroin, right-wing politics, clergy demagoguery, or booze. For freedom, Christ has set us free, so that we might be captivated by Christ.

FAITH

Acknowledgement that what scripture says is happening, actually is. Willingness to be whom God has created us to be; readiness to be transformed and transfigured by someone who works beyond, beneath, and above things as they seem to our senses. More a welcoming wave than a stiff salute, when Christ turns to us. Paying attention. Overcome by light. Enraptured.

Faith happens when reality, first experienced as mundane and speechless, overflows, so that we hear something and exclaim, "I believe." Better than some innate human yearning, faith is our reasonable response to an occurrence that has happened to us, named Jesus Christ. More than intellectual assent, the Christian faith is about walking with Christ even when you aren't sure where he's taking you. Being faithful more than having faith.

Faith arises when we begin to trust Jesus more than ourselves. Most of us come to trust the God that Christianity talks about before we sign up for the whole system. Once you take that first trusting step toward the God who turns to you, Christian teaching, beliefs, and behavior begin to make sense.

Jesus asked a man born blind, whom he has just healed, whether or not he "believes" in the Human One (or Son of Man). Jesus isn't asking the man if he thinks that Jesus exists—Jesus stands in front of him. Jesus is asking if the healed person is ready to trust the one he is staring at. The man responds simply, "I believe." When a gang of religious scholars gives the man hell for saying he believes in Jesus, the man replies, "Don't know much 'bout theology. All I know was I once was blind but now I see." This dynamic—believing before all the evidence is in—occurs in the souls of millions.

We are saved "through faith," which sounds to us pragmatic, mother-I'd-rather-do it-myself Americans like another assignment for self-betterment. No, faith is a gift. Not what we should, ought, must but rather God's having done, finished, given. If we can say, "I trust Christ," it's a sure sign that God has made good on God's electing promise: I will be your God; you will be my people.

Paul says that Abraham (who wasn't a Christian) is the prime exemplar of faith. Old Abram saddling up the camels, his geriatric wife pregnant, heading out on the basis of a cockeyed promise from a God he had only recently, briefly met. Abraham and Sarah are about as good examples of faith as we've got.

However, Jesus repeatedly rebukes his disciples for their lack of faith, little faith, slow faith, and inability to believe what prophets said about him. Fortunately, we don't need much of it; faith the size of a mustard seed will do. Bring on those mountains.

"Faith" categorized as a generic human tendency is insipid. Everything depends on what you have faith in. The bland expressions "people of faith" or "faith community" presume that all faiths are the same and that there are people who have "faith" and people who don't. When someone says, "I don't have faith in Christ," it means, not that they are faithless but rather that they have put their faith in someone other than a Jew from Nazareth who lived briefly, died violently, and rose unexpectedly. When free-floating "faith" becomes "faith in Christ," that's when our lackluster little lives become adventurous and talk of "faith" becomes interesting.

Have trouble trusting that Christ is the truth about God? Be patient. Faith comes to you rather than you to it. The God whom you have difficulty turning toward has promised to turn toward you. Besides, who wants a God who is no more than the one you chose?

FALL

Some say that when once innocent Adam and Eve ate the forbidden fruit, humanity fell into sin, and thereby infected forever the human race. While it's debatable that the book of Genesis sees it that way, it's a fact that the very first opportunity we had to go our way rather than God's, we did. It's been downhill ever since.

God has graciously created us free to choose to be who we have been created to be. Yet choice isn't real if it's not freedom to choose to disobey. And disobey we do. We can sincerely want to do what is right yet be powerless to do it. Though we have been given freedom, we are caught in a web of desires, deceits, biases, and inclinations that sure feels like we've fallen a long way below what we're meant to be. We need saving from ourselves. A fresh start. Clean slate. Support. Rebirth.

None of which, fallen as we are, can we do by ourselves.

FORGIVENESS

God's costly response to human evil; Christ's expectation for how we are to respond to those who do evil to us.

Israel discovered that God was very patient, quick to forgive, and limitless in faithful love for the ungodly, unkind, and selfish. Not what we expected from so holy, righteous, and demanding a God.

Forgiveness is God's self-definition. That's why Jesus never gave a utilitarian justification for forgiveness, such as, "By forgiving someone you will bring out the best in that wrongdoer and may even lower your blood pressure." Christ said that we ought to treat others like God has treated us. We are obliged to be forgivers by worshipping a Lord who looks down from the cross upon which we nailed him and said, "Father, forgive."

Questions:

What if the person who has wronged us is unrepentant? Although repentance is the right thing to do when we've wronged someone, it's annoying that Jesus usually practiced preemptive forgiveness, forgiving people before they asked, absolving them of their sin before they knew they were sinners. Perhaps the ability to tell the truth about ourselves follows, rather than precedes, forgiveness.

Though it's possible to forgive without the other confessing, it's hard to imagine the relationship restored if there's no honest admission of the wrong that was done after forgiveness is offered. Sometimes we forgive, without receiving confession or apology, because it's too big a burden to continue to hold on to the wrong that was done. Another's inability to confess ought not restrain our ability to respond as Christ commands. Painful though it is when someone refuses to accept our forgiveness, at least we know how God feels.

Is it wrong to want vengeance? A desire for repayment of the debt owed to you is a sign that the relationship mattered and that the sin is serious. But retribution can also imprison you, letting the wrong done to you define you. When you have suffered a great injustice, it's doubtful that even the most severe retribution extracted from a wrongdoer will bring closure to your pain. More importantly, God says "vengeance is mine," not yours. Some wrong is so wrong that only God can do justice for the victim and the victimizer. "Let me handle this," says Jesus, taking the task of payback off your back.

As difficult as it is to forgive someone who has wronged you, why is it sometimes more difficult to receive than to offer forgiveness? It's forgiveness. Who wants to be indebted to someone who has experienced you at your worst, suffered at your hands, and still forgives you for it?

Should all wrong against us be forgiven? To do so could have deleterious, long-term consequences. In no way does forgiveness imply that the injustice was inconsequential. Still, seemingly unconcerned about the possible detrimental effects of too much forgiveness given too freely, Jesus commanded us to love our enemies and to forgive not once, not twice, but seventy times seven, which is a whole heap of forgiveness. "Unforgiveable" is not an expression Jesus used except when he said that all sins can be forgiven except "sin against the Holy Spirit." Fortunately, nobody knows what Jesus meant by that.

I know I must forgive, but must I forgive right now? It takes time for trust to be rebuilt, even when the breach has been forgiven. In commanding us to forgive seventy times seven, Jesus depicts forgiveness as more than a heroic, momentary act. In Matthew 18 Jesus offers a step-by-step process for when someone has wronged you, culminating in asking the whole church for help with the heavy lifting. Sometimes it's better to say, "I'm on the way to forgiving you," than "I have forgiven."

Forgive and forget? Forgetting could imply that the wrong that was done wasn't all that wrong. Forgiveness sometimes says, "Though I will always remember this wound, I will, by forgiving you, go on. The wound will not wholly determine us." Rarely does forgiveness bring about "closure" or take you back to "where we were." Though we can't forget, at least we can be unstuck and on our way to a different future than we would have had if we had not been obedient to Jesus.

When we say, as we must while walking with Jesus, "Lord be merciful to me a sinner," sometimes the mercy we seek is Christ's forgiveness for our being unable to forgive.

GOD

Whoever brought Israel out of slavery and raised crucified Jesus from the dead.

God is not a description of a generic, big, distant, omnipotent, indefinable something but the name of a personal, active, resourceful someone. A babe in Bethlehem whose birth elicited affection, worship, trouble, pain, and violence is God's self-definition and self-revelation, as much of God as we hope to see in this world. God on a cross is God being most godly. The one God is the relentlessly relational Father to whom we pray, the demanding, revealing Son in whose name we cry out, the dynamic, intrusive Holy Spirit who teaches us how to talk to God.

"Give us word of yourself," we asked God down through the ages. "Don't be coy. Tell us who you are and what you are up to." God decisively turned toward us saying, "Jesus Christ."

GOSPEL

Good news about something that's happened, events that we don't come up with on our own.

Our challenge has always been not to pervert God's good news into the bad news of just another scheme for saving ourselves by ourselves. Thus, God's good news implies the bad news of judgment upon all human attempts to hoist ourselves up to God. Good news can be bad news: it all depends on what you're up to when you get the news.

Ask people, "What is the gospel?" Many will reply, "I must believe that Jesus died for my sins so that when I die my soul can go to heaven." Jesus becomes the passive automaton who was briefly among us and trudged to his death so that we win our ticket to eternity. Too much is left out: Jesus's life is detached from his death, and Christ's salvation becomes your personal quiz that, if passed, leads to the optimum individual destination. Do this, God will give you that, our relationship with God a transaction that's dependent upon our astute believing, wise deciding, or good behaving. This, good news?

Good news: our relationship with God is God's self-assigned task. "This is our message—God is light!" What must you do? Let Jesus shine on you so that he can then shine in the world through you.

The good news is that Jesus wants more than a "personal relationship" with you. He is Lord, satisfied with nothing less than being light for the whole darkened world.

GOSPELS

Carefully crafted narratives, sermons, really, that—just like your walk with Christ—have a beginning, middle, and end.

Somebody named Mark, sometime during the first century, somewhere in the Levant, invented a literary form as a means of recruitment into the Jesus movement. Biography (sort of), travel saga (of a kind), more of a sermon than a news report or historical account, Mark's Gospel is a distinctively narrative way of presenting a unique messiah.

The truth about Jesus required more than one of these Gospels to do justice to the complexity of the subject. Four distinctive voices, each offering a rambunctious travelogue replete with excursions such as, "Jesus told this parable to certain people who had convinced themselves that they were righteous and who looked on everyone else with disgust." Ouch.

The church is not self-generated but rather arises as a response to a fourfold script that requires regular reiteration. The Gospels want to enable Jesus, teller of tales, to become the master story that subsumes our stories. As we read ourselves into his story, Jesus writes himself into the world, and the tales of God-with-Us continue.

GRACE

Gift. God's love in action.

No innocuous pat on the head as Jesus murmurs unctuously, "I love you just the way you are; promise me you won't change a thing." Grace is how Christ, in the power of the Holy Spirit, appears to us and works for us and in us. Grace comes in at least three ways. In the cross and resurrection of Jesus, God deals with the dissonance between you and God (justifying grace). In subtle, often unknown means God maneuvers, intrudes, and comes to you before you know it's God (prevenient grace). God continues to work in you to draw you closer (sanctification). By grace, you're given a more amazing life than the one you thought you were fated to live.

HEALING

What God does: sometimes as a surprising, undeserved intervention, sometimes working through the skilled hands and hearts of those who are called by God to the vocation of health care.

To pray for healing from illness is to admit that your recovery is mostly out of your hands.

Though the Lord's Prayer forgets to mention health and healing, it's okay to pray for healing—as long as you note that in scripture, prayer is for more than wellness. Today, most prayers are for health, because it's the only thing left for God to do now that we are gods unto ourselves. It's not enough that God has given us life; we want life without pain or limitation. Trouble is, bodily deterioration is the long-term cost incurred for being human.

While obsession with physical health is now praised as prudential "self-care," more than we like to admit, some of our health problems are our fault—bad lifestyle choices, refusal to wear a mask during a pandemic, a failure to take responsibility for the bodies God has given us, a repudiation of God's creation of us as creatures.

Jesus occasionally healed and still heals: what God is up to now, albeit intermittently in this world, a foretaste of what will one day be forever. Sometimes, when Jesus healed someone, he strictly charged them to tell nobody. Jesus has a greater mission than delivering good medical care. Jesus is better even than a doctor.

Be warned: Jesus doesn't wait until we get better—in body, mind, or spirit—to summon us to discipleship and give us work. Even from your deathbed, he expects witness, suggesting that if there's one thing worse than a dearth of good health it's lack of vocation.

Physical health is a good, as far as it goes (never far enough to satisfy our desire for immortality). Sickness is a hint of what lies ahead. Everybody who was healed by Jesus, even his friend Lazarus, died. Once, the church was the most prominent, overly built, and least effective building in town. Now, it's the hospital. Weirdly dressed clergy have been replaced by folks in scrubs and white coats. Much that passes for "health care" today has become "immortality fantasy management."

Worship of physical health and a well-toned physique, medical practices that promise total avoidance of pain or sure-fire fixing of our bad lifestyle choices, and indefinite prolongation of bodily existence at any cost, find no friend in Jesus.

HEAVEN

Paradise. God with us; we with God, forever.

As Jesus hung on the cross, one of the thieves hanging next to him pled, "Jesus, remember me when you come into your kingdom." The wretched man was surely thinking of tomorrow. Today, with Jesus in agony on the cross, mocked by a howling mob, deserted by his followers, any promised "kingdom" must be a faraway future.

Jesus surprised him: "Today you will be with me in paradise." You might expect Jesus to say, "Someday—if you truly believe in me, repent and get your life together—you will be with me in paradise. Just you wait."

No, Jesus said, "Today you will be with me in paradise."

If Jesus had been walking along some Galilean road in the bright sunshine, rather than hanging on a cross under darkening sky, I believe this conversation would have gone the same way. "Paradise" isn't a place where we might go someday if we are good; it begins today, as Jesus turns toward us and we felons turn toward Jesus. Heaven is more than our time extended and made better; heaven is Jesus giving eternal life to anyone he wants.

Christians believe in eternal life, not based upon who we are or what we have done—some divine spark, an eternal kernel in us that goes on and on, immortality—but because of what we believe about God. Having raised crucified Jesus, God triumphs over death, giving hope to any who suffer and die. And don't we all?

"Because I live, you will live too," not only then and there but here and now.

Many of Jesus's parables have as their theme, "Ready or not, here comes the kingdom of heaven." Heaven is both the future of the believer and place from which Jesus will come to judge.

Paul calls us naturalized citizens of heaven. Christians have dual citizenship. "Here we have no lasting city, but we are looking for the city that is to come." We ought not to take this world too seriously. While there's a "now" and "not yet" quality to heaven, hope of heaven in the future affects life here and now. Learn to be with God now so that you will be ready to live with God forever, says the church. Service in Sunday worship and Monday through Saturday service to the world are rehearsals for when we'll eternally whoop it up in God's heavenly choir.

If you think of heaven as an exclusive gated community, take note: heaven is well populated—a vast banquet, a wedding feast, an innumerable multitude convened by God, a city—New Jerusalem—whose limits are unknown to us.

After a lecture, Karl Barth was asked, "Do you think we'll see again those we love in heaven?" Barth replied, "Yes, I do. And those we hate."

Heaven is God's will being done. "I saw a new heaven and a new earth, for the former heaven and the former earth had passed away, and the sea was no more. I saw the holy city, New Jerusalem, coming down out of heaven from God, made ready as a bride beautifully dressed for her husband. . . . Look! God's dwelling is here with humankind. He will dwell with them, and they will be his peoples. God himself will be with them as their God." It's restoration of the relationship with God that we once knew in the garden, now known forever in God's capacious city.

The Bible doesn't talk about "going to heaven when you die." It talks about God remaking this world, a new creation. Christian faith practiced here, now, readies for life when God's new creation shall be our home.

More Americans are believing in the afterlife while fewer believe in God—who could deny immortality to people who are so nice? If heaven is being in the eternal presence of God, wouldn't heaven be hell if you've spent your life trying to get rid of God?

Those of us who make a living keeping up earthly temples, parish churches, and university chapels are unnerved to learn that in heaven there is no temple. Presumably, there'll be no priests either because then, everybody's a priest prancing around God's altar. God will not dwell in a temple served by a few ecclesiastical functionaries; God will reign throughout the whole city, praised by a multitudinous choir made up of every creature. We won't need to get dressed and come to a church at an undesirable hour to be with God; God will have gotten to us.

As Jesus waltzed into paradise after his resurrection and ascension, surely his Father asked, "What have you got to show for all your trouble and pain? Where are the citizens of your kingdom?" Christ produced as his trophy one slightly informed, somewhat repentant thief.

HELL

When we are at last left alone, consumed by the fires of our egotism, the snake eating its tail, at last able to say triumphantly, "I'll be damned before I'll let you love me."

A belief in hell requires a leap of faith. Though there's little biblical evidence that human stupidity overpowers God's mercy, maybe it is possible for humans forever to thwart God's purposes. However, if you have had firsthand experience of God turning toward you, refusing to leave you safe in your loneliness, it's hard to imagine Jesus saying, "That's it. I give up. To hell with 'em."

That's why we can't say much for sure about hell, far less than we can say about heaven; our eternal destiny is up to God rather than us. It's hard to imagine a time or place where ubiquitous God is not. Christians tend to be agnostic about the existence of hell and damnation, not because people are basically good and don't deserve an eternal thrashing, but because God is eternally resourceful, deep in mercy. That's why many of the faithful have said, "Hell? No."

If there is a hell, it must be smaller even than Lichtenstein, considering how much territory is claimed by Jesus. The church has always taught that there was a hell, but has never said who was in it. If the church can't say for sure that even Judas is in hell, we are justified in the hope that if there is a hell, it could be empty.

HERESY

A personal opinion; fruit of a fertile imagination that refuses to believe what the church has, at all times and places believed.

Heresy is a progressivist self-delusion that your knowledge of God is better than your grandmother's: usually, the same old wrong idea dressed in new garb.

Most heresies tend to be oversimplifications, sincere pastoral attempts to tidy up doctrine, facile resolutions of the fierce tensions inherent in the orthodox belief that a crucified Jew is as much of God as we'll ever know.

The church hopes that all Christian doctrine and proclamation arise out of and then remains answerable to scripture. In church history, heretics tend to be interesting, though overly impressed by their own creativity. Orthodoxy is humble and unassuming, content to wrestle with what God has told us, modestly allowing Jesus to be as simple and straightforward and as unmanageable and ineffable as he pleases.

HOLY

Commandeered by God for Godly purposes.

Pots, pans, scrolls, and buildings can be holy when utilized by God in God's turning toward us. For some reason a circumcised penis is a sign of Israel's holiness; only God knows why. Paul says that Christ requisitions even our frail mortal bodies as holy temples.

True, you can worship God just about anywhere. But there do seem to be peculiarly holy places like little rural churches, prison cells, forlorn church camps, and books by C. S. Lewis or Marilynne Robinson where, for reasons known only to God, God shows up. Since Jesus died and rose for everybody, particularly holy people, sometimes famous, most of them you've never heard of, have been shining exemplars—sometimes forlorn, ragged ones—whom God grabs for God's purposes: all, saints.

Once the Hebrews get to Mount Sinai, Yahweh explains that they were delivered from enslavement to the Egyptians in order to requisition them to do unpaid work for God as a holy people, a nation of priests. First Peter proclaims, "You are a chosen people, a royal priesthood, a holy nation, God's special possession, that you may declare the praises of him who called you out of darkness into his wonderful light." In Christ, all the baptized are priests calling all the world to worship.

Experience of the holy is the awe-filled recognition of God's otherness. When the truth of Jesus's messianic identity came to Simon Peter, his first reaction was, "Get away from me! I'm a sinful man!" In

2 Samuel 6, Uzzah attempted to steady the chest containing God's covenant and paid with his life. Divine holiness cannot be managed.

God descends Mount Sinai in order to give the Hebrews their marching orders. Moses warns Israel to wash its clothes and not go near the mountain (or be stoned to death or shot with arrows) because holy God is descending. It's dangerous to try to get too cozy with God, though it's okay for the holy God to come down to us.

Little wonder that some clergy, though ordained to bring us before the holy, instead offer their congregations folksy, chatty, smarmy, profane protection from God. When was the last time Sunday morning worship scared the hell out of you?

HOLY SPIRIT

Pneuma. *Wind. In stable, stolid, mainline, North American Protestantism, the most neglected member of the Trinity. Antithesis of the human spirit. God made contemporary, revealed, in motion toward us here, now.*

When we first meet the Holy Spirit in Genesis we find the Spirit hovering over the waters to give life, to bring forth something out of chaotic nothing. The Holy Spirit intrudes into an otherwise dull church meeting at Pentecost and we discover that the Holy Spirit is not only creative and life-giving but also incendiary and disruptive. Foundations shake. Fire descends. Once silenced people now do the talking. Only the Spirit who created the world can birth a church.

A favorite work of the Holy Spirit is the incitement of speech, hearing, and comprehension, which is why it's customary to pray before scripture is read and proclaimed, "Holy Spirit, come on down! Tell us things we could never tell ourselves! Break through the barriers we've built between God's speaking and our hearing. Bring it on, Holy Spirit!"

Discipleship and witness are not self-sustainable. Like air filling our lungs, the Spirit of God refreshes, partnering with us in our vocation to speak up for God, enabling us to join in God's work. Close your life to the inspiration of the Holy Spirit and the result is stolidity, suffocation, silence.

Thus we are told that when we are dragged into court, victims of lordless authorities, we're not to worry about preparation. "The Holy Spirit will teach you at that very hour what you are to say." Paul goes so far as to claim that no one can say, "Jesus is Lord" except by the prompting of the Holy Spirit.

When Jesus was baptized the Holy Spirit descended upon his body "like a dove," a voice announced, "You are my Son, the beloved, with whom I'm well pleased."

In the power of the Holy Spirit, Jesus preached his first sermon in Nazareth, announcing the emptying of prisons and good news for those who had, before Jesus, heard nothing but bad news. And then, as sometimes happens with the descent of the Holy Spirit and Spirit-induced speech, the congregation exploded and tried to kill the preacher. Sadly, the church convened by the Holy Spirit can also be a clever defense against it.

Better than an impersonal, vague force, the Holy Spirit is a personality that loves to create, to initiate, to bring something new out of something old, to shake things up, to give possibility and create potentiality in times and places where we thought we were at a dead end. Creating, speaking and hearing, preaching that wallops, and yes, disrupting our placid present with God's lively, unexpected future are only some of the Holy Spirit's shenanigans.

One can be "spiritual" without being in the spirit of Jesus. We must test the spirits. If it's the Holy Spirit, it's the spirit of Jesus. Paul lists the Spirit's fruits as "love, joy, peace, patience, kindness, goodness, faithfulness, gentleness, and self-control." To which I add holy disruption, dislodgement, dissonance, and dislocation.

HUMILITY

Close cousin of "humus" and, after Jesus, "human." What separates Jesus from other kings.

Though he could have chinned up to our definitions of God Almighty, Jesus chose humility. For followers of Jesus, humility is what the world does to us rather than a spiritual virtue worked up by us.

"You must turn and become as a little child" seems an odd saying. Ever tried to be small?

Walk with Jesus long enough, the world will find a way to humble you. Tough (if you are into maturity, popularity, and fame) but good news: your downward descent puts you not far from the kingdom. Thus, while humiliation is always degrading, and, well, humiliating, for any of its pain, God uses our humbling as opportunity to turn ever closer toward us. Nobody gets near a crucified God without some stooping.

The world curses or, at least, ridicules the humble; Jesus castigates the proud, notices the downcast, and blesses the "poor in spirit," drawing to himself all the spiritually inept, incompetent, and deficient, so often looked down upon by the spiritually adept.

"When you come in glory, who will get to sit next to you in majesty?" we asked at his Last Supper. Jesus takes a bowl and towel, washes our feet and says, "Now, you try it."

We look up and shout to God, "Tear open the heavens and come down!" only to look down and see God Almighty kneeling at our feet.

Every time we're humbled by the judgments of God, our critics, or the results of our stupidity, we come undone and are pushed back, for a moment, to the world pre–Genesis 1. If it weren't for God's gifting creativity in making humanity out of mud, we would be nothing. Humility teaches that for all our virtues and competences we are not God: we are humus, living on borrowed breath.

Also humbling that, for all of our all-too-human weaknesses, God chose humble us to turn the world upside down so that God could put it right side up.

HUMOR

Not a traditional Christian virtue, though I fail to see why.

You don't think of church as fun or clergy as funny. God laughs on only one occasion, hooting at politicians. And though we don't see Jesus laugh, his knuckleheaded disciples surely gave someone as merciful with human foibles and frailty as Jesus multiple opportunities to smirk, "Are you kidding me?"

When very old Sarah is told that she is to be very pregnant with her first child, Sarah lets out a toothless laugh. Interrogated by God, she lies that she laughed. Nine months later, little Isaac ("Laughter") is born. Don't tell me God doesn't have a sense of humor.

Jesus's characteristic mode of communicating was through parables, first cousin of jokes. On the road to Jericho a man is beaten and left half dead in the ditch. He is bypassed by devout, religious people, clergy and lay. The only one who stops and extravagantly helps? A no-good Samaritan.

The joke is on us.

Whether or not the Gospel writers intended to be humorous or satirical, I know not. Yet I find therein some great comedic moments. Jesus comes upon a crippled man who has been lying by a magic pool for thirty-eight years, waiting on an angel to heal him. Jesus asks, "Would you like to be healed?"

The forgotten punch line: "In lying here for thirty-eight years, the thought has occurred to me."

After seeing the empty tomb, John says the disciples "returned to their homes." These clowns could witness a resurrection and still not let it interfere with brunch.

Hear the one about the Son of God who came to us with good news so we crucified him? Better to laugh than to cry.

In his most famous sermon, Jesus tells those who have tears today, they'll have laughter tomorrow. Is that why some of the church fathers characterized Easter as "the joke played on the devil"?

HUNGER

We don't live by bread alone, but we don't live long without it; thus, "daily bread" is one of the few gifts Jesus permits us to ask for in the Lord's Prayer.

Hunger motivates some of our worst behavior. Adam and Eve's stomachs got the best of them as they looked, desired, took, and ate. The rest is human history. Jacob tricks his older brother out of his birthright using nothing more than a bowl of good smelling red stew. Once aroused, our appetites make us stupid.

As soon as the Hebrews were free from slavery and in the wilderness, their stomachs growled. They whined, "At least in Egypt we had three square meals a day." God got angry at their ingratitude, but cooled down. When the people woke the next morning, the ground was covered in bread from heaven.

As they tasted the manna they asked, "What is it?" I'll tell you: it's a merciful God giving God's people what they need to make it through the wilderness on the way to the land of milk and honey.

Jesus blessed the hungering and the thirsting, telling them that now that he's here, they'll be filled. When Jesus encountered the famished multitudes, he ordered his disciples, "You give them something to eat." Then he took the little they had, blessed, broke, and gave it (a fourfold table action you've seen on many a Sunday).

Manna all over again. Enough bread for all, even in the wilderness, because of Jesus.

Jesus not only fed hungry people but commanded his followers to do the same, making bread a spiritual issue. From the first, imperial Romans were baffled by how Christians fed the hungry, even those who weren't part of the church.

Define blasphemy? One hungry child.

We had gathered at table for a civil, balanced, intellectual discussion of spiritual matters, only to have Jesus blurt out, "Feed on me! Wolf down my body and gulp my blood as if it were your last meal! I don't want just your thoughts and feelings: I desire all of you, soul and body, and I want you to ingest all of me!"

The night before his trial and death, Jesus gathered with his friends, who were soon to be his betrayers, picked up a loaf of bread and said, "This is what it's all about. This is what I'm up to from here to eternity. Have some bread. Take some wine."

IDOLATRY

Obeisance to a fake god of our concoction, fabrication of a godlet easier to live with than Father, Son, and Holy Spirit.

We are incurably spiritual, pious eager beavers who fervently bow down and worship anything if given half a chance to worship something. Though idolatry at first seems easier than worship of the Trinity, failing to give God glory has its price. With so much bowing and scraping before the tyrannical idols of flag, dollar, popularity, or financial security, lower back pain is endemic. Call it what you want, but whatever you sacrifice your children for, that's your god. The question is not "Will you worship?" but "Whom?"

The Hebrews are liberated from Egyptian enslavement. Moses treks up Sinai to ask God for direction. No sooner than Moses leaves the camp, everybody gets organized, tosses in their looted Egyptian jewelry, and a gold calf is produced. The band strikes up and the service begins with repetitious praise choruses. Let the utilization of the divine commence!

Moses—and the Lord—go ballistic when they see all Israel cavorting around the calf.

Aaron defends them: "They needed a boost. Something positive. Unity. The parking lot is full, the budget up, so we must be doing something right."

Politics has forged the gold calf of the moment. The first Christians weren't persecuted for worship of Christ; they were martyred for refusing to worship Caesar. Satan tempts Jesus in the wilderness by offering him lordship over the governments of the world, the power to do good! All Jesus must do is worship Satan.

When Paul addresses the Athenians, he does so as a faithful Jew who knows violation of the first commandment when he sees it: "People of Athens, I see that you are very religious in every way." Poor Gentiles, they think Paul is paying them a compliment.

It's natural for us pagans to put something else in place of the God we've got, some dead god (i.e., idol) who never surprises. Unnatural is worship of a God as judgmental as Jesus. Patriotism comes as naturally as love of family—especially adoration of one's grandchildren—crafty cover for adoration of ourselves; love of Jesus takes training.

White skin, white power, white pride, and white identity are more serious than merely sociological, psychological, economic mistakes. They are God substitutes in whose worship is death. Beware: Israel's God is jealous, intolerant of any godlet who messes with God's property that God paid for in blood.

IMMORTAL

Death-proof (which we aren't). Nothing about us is built to last.

Grief at the death of someone we love is for good reason. Death sucks. Avoidance of funerals suggests an unwillingness to think about the possibility that, for all of our virtues, all that we love, including ourselves, shall be ripped off.

When it comes to dealing with death, sentimental bromides like, "She will live on in our memories," or "His accomplishments shall last forever," fail to lift the luggage. Wishful thinking that something about us goes on—immortal soul, indomitable human spirit, best-selling author (!), persistence of memory and love—is no match for the desolation of death.

Our hope is not in the resolute human spirit but in God's indefatigable determination to have us. Knowing that in Christ God loves to rob the "final enemy" of victory, we trust that the One who was raised from the dead shall take us along for the ride.

INCARNATION

What God did at Christmas. The enfleshment of God. Divine condescension to humanity through Mary's womb. Transcendence upended by what happens in Jesus. The lengths God is willing to go to have us.

From the first, we watched Jesus do what humans do (hunger, bleed, grieve, rejoice) and also that which only God can do (forgiving sins or routing demons).

The first Christian martyr Stephen addresses his prayers not as he has been taught—to Adonai—but to Jesus, "Lord Jesus, receive my spirit," speaking to Jesus just like Israel prayed to God. Jesus recognized as divine is not something that was added to Jesus by his overly enthusiastic followers, but there from the first, right after his resurrection and ascension.

The first commandment strictly prohibits making representations of Almighty God. But it's okay if God wants to make an image of God.

The incarnation says in the flesh what the prophets, patriarchs, and matriarchs tried to tell us: God doesn't float over our chaos, pain, and sin, nor reside safely among our ancestors amid the dead. God personally wants to meet us not only here but also now. God risks relationship, dares to give Godself into human hands, becomes a body. No woozy mysticism, high-flown idealism, or fuzzy spirirualty adequately describes the God who not only invented flesh but also became our flesh.

Only God can save us. Only God has eternity. And yet, humanity can't be fully redeemed if God is unwilling to assume full humanity. If Christ is only human, he is irrelevant to deepest human need and can't be worshipped. If he is only God, then he is disconnected from human limitations and can't be followed.

Jesus is the key to God's nature and intentions. Everything about God is embodied in him; Jesus is God both supremely and uniquely at work. Jesus doesn't just make God visible but actively present. Jesus, the supreme instance of God's agency. God is so determined to self-reveal that God gives us a human life who shows what God wants to happen, and who makes possible for us to want God.

Around academia, on rare moments when God creeps into conversation, there's always someone around to say, "God? Can't say much for sure. God is large, distant, unknowable. It would be intellectually constricting and presumptuous to claim knowledge of God."

We wish.

Jesus as fully God and fully human is a paradox, yes, but he is also a lovable person. Who warms to a paradox? When you love someone, you embrace that person's wild oppositional complexity, seemingly paradoxical behavior makes you love your friend all the more. Jesus Christ seems paradoxical only to those who think God and humanity are mutually exclusive.

Sweet, well-meaning religious folk are forever trying to overspiritualize God, filling the faith with helium and floating it up toward never-never-land. In the incarnation, we learn that bodies matter; matter matters. Heaven and earth are interlocked, embraced. God doesn't snatch us from this fallen creation, leaving the wretched world behind. The world, our world, is entered into, intertwined with God's purposes.

Incarnation is best used as a noun rather than as an adjective or adverb. "Incarnational ministry" doesn't say much; all humans are meaty. Incarnation means more than "Human existence is good and therefore ought to be embraced and improved" (people on top always think that). Incarnation is a Jew from Nazareth who lived briefly, died violently, rose unexpectedly, and was God.

If you prefer your God to be with you as a remarkably effective moral teacher or a wise sage, Jesus is sure to discomfort. The domesticated Jesus whose strange, inextricable mix of humanity and divinity has somehow been made simpler—either human or divine; hence easy for us to understand and to handle—is no Christ at all. The incarnation beckons us toward intellectual humility, a willingness to let God be at the same time mysteriously complicated, beyond the bounds of our full comprehension, and yet closer to us than we are to ourselves.

On the other hand, if you prefer your God shrouded in spiritual, inflated, pale blue, fuzzy vagueness, far removed from where you actually reside, irrelevant to who you really are, Jesus's human nearness will be unnerving.

In its orthodox thinking about the incarnation, the church allowed God to stoop as low as God pleased and at the same time to exalt humanity as high as God wanted. But some tried to come up with simpler, less paradoxical, less demanding formulations for the God/Man Jesus:

Adoptionism: Jesus is a fine human being who, empowered by the Holy Spirit, became (maybe at his baptism) like the prophets of the Old Testament, but even better. Through his adoption by God, Jesus is a very powerful, very good human being: almost God, but not quite.

Docetism: Jesus is totally divine and only appeared to be human. Christ presented himself to humanity in a human costume. A lot like us, but not quite.

Arianism: God is transcendent and holy and can't be too close to the human without degrading God's divinity. Even though Jesus Christ is not divine, he is the absolute highest and best creation who ever was. Human, but not quite; God, but not quite. God has not sullied God's godliness by descending to us, but by taking Christ as our model, we can ascend toward God.

To all these heresies, orthodox Christians have said that what God has not assumed can't be healed. A Jesus distant from either God or humanity can't save. The doctrine of the incarnation is the church's attempt to talk about what countless Christians have found true: God has turned to us, a turning that's typical of a God who from the first, shows up, who won't let us alone, no matter how much it costs.

Moses is told that nobody can look upon the face of God and live. Because of Christ, now you can.

ISRAEL

Contenders against God; God's beloved people.

Jacob was on the lam after jilting his brother out of his inheritance. By the River Jabbok, a mysterious stranger jumps Jacob and they wrestle all night. At dawn, when Jacob finally pins his adversary, he demands a blessing. "You've struggled with God and with men and won," says the stranger. "Your name won't be Jacob any longer, but Israel the God-wrestler." Jacob went on to become the father of a great people, though he always walked with a limp.

God never got over God's inclination to wrestle Israel. "I will be your God and you will be my people." We can all be grateful that God loves to tussle intransigents into an enduring relationship.

God's arguments with Israel become quickly overheated—God has bet the house on Israel—so much is at stake. When Israel is faithful, Yahweh looks good. When Israel doesn't do well, God looks like a sucker for steadfastly loving such losers, which of course God is. The prophets continue God's lover's quarrel with Israel, confident that one day, everybody will come to Zion, drawn by Israel, God's beloved showcase, sign to all the nations of what God can do when God promises to love a people, no matter their contentiousness.

The best we Gentiles can hope for is to be adopted, by baptism, as honorary Jews, members of an expanded Israel, contentious combatants, wrestled into God's faithful love.

JESUS

Christianity is about the Jew, Jesus. An historical figure but more.

Jesus is the irreducible stuff of the Christian faith, the test for all the church says about what it believes. Because of the words and deeds in the Gospels and Paul's Letters (the most reliable early sources for thinking about Jesus), we can't make God anything we please.

From the first, Jesus failed to meet our expectations for how a savior ought to save us. We tried to use Jesus to get what we want only to have Jesus enlist us to get what God wants.

It's always a challenge to love and to live with the God we've got rather than the one we just had to have. Jesus apparently wants both a personal relationship with you, even you, as well as lordship over the whole cosmos and everybody else.

One more thing about Jesus: he's alive, present, bodily present. (What sort of "presence" is there that's not bodily?) He not only spoke but speaks. He once worked signs and wonders and is still at it.

Note: in spite of what this book might lead you to believe, having the right words about Jesus is not as important as having a relationship with Jesus, God turned toward you, no matter the cost.

JOY

According to Revelation, the main business of heaven.

The Westminster Confession asserts that joy is the point of your life. You are here for no better purpose than to "glorify and to en*joy* God forever."

When angels fill the heavens announcing to shepherds working the night shift—"I bring good news to you—wonderful, joyous news for all people. Your savior is born today"—we are reminded that the joy of a Christian is responsive to an unexpected gift.

After a long lecture and a series of demanding commands Jesus asserts, "I have said these things to you so that my joy will be in you and your joy will be complete." Apparently, Jesus's is not your run-of-the-mill notion of joy.

Virtue or vice? Depends on what causes it. While smashing one's enemies can bring joy, and amassing lots of cash can be gleeful, instead, Paul exhorts to "rejoice in the Lord always," probably writing from a jail cell where he awaited execution. Christian joy is weird.

JUDGMENT

Accountability. A consequence of being loved by a God who gives a damn.

In key moments (such as when Jesus appeared before Pilate or was cross-examined by religious scholars), the world put Jesus on trial only to have him turn the tables and judge the world.

God gets angry not because God is wrathful by nature but because God cares. While God is slow to anger, a few things make God's blood boil: injustice, idolatry, and infidelity, for starters. On at least one occasion God goes so far as to hate. The reason? Worship gone bad. Rather than wonder why Jesus angrily turned over the tables and whipped the money changers out of the temple, better to ask, "Why we are so calm and collected in the face of evil?"

Christ's judgmentalism is a function of his having entrusted to us the display of his kingdom. Jesus told a number of parables that have as their theme, *What have you done with what you have been given?*

Why doesn't God just let us be? Having given us the good news, God holds us accountable for giving it to others. God's gifts are God's assignments. Jesus takes it personally when we give him a poor return on his investment. Christ actually believes that we can grow to be faithful disciples. There's no getting better without accountability. Judgment and grace, anger and love: different sides of the same God.

When we pray, "Thy kingdom come, thy will be done," what did we expect? There's no justice without adjudication. No love without indignation when that love is betrayed. Angry judgment against the privileged and the powerful, the rich and the hypocritical, is one way God cares for the poor and the dispossessed. I may not be courageous or indignant enough to set all things right, but be well assured that someday, somehow, the Judge will.

BTW: My judgment on myself, your verdict on me, and my assessment of you are not the final word on me or you. The last word is

God's. Just remember: the one who sits upon the throne, separating the sheep from the goats, is the judge who was judged in our place, Christ.

JUSTICE

The psalmist sings that eventually justice and mercy kiss; these days they hardly speak.

It's delicious to believe that someday the people who have wronged you will get what they deserve; not so much fun is to believe that you also shall be judged.

At various times, Jesus was dragged before the agents of justice, both religious Caiaphas and secular Pontius Pilate. One of the noblest systems of justice responded to Jesus by torturing him to death. Worldly attempts at justice usually involve the strong imposing their will upon the weak. In crying out for justice, the weak demand power to work their will upon the strong. Maybe that's why, in world history, Jesus is usually on the losing side. After the revolution, who can distinguish the vanquished, morally speaking, from the victors? People with power act the same, no matter how they got it. All of which explains why Jesus never gets along with potentates, religious or otherwise.

There are unjust situations that we can't put right and wounds of injustice that we can't heal. (1) We can't make the wrong that has been done not to have been. (2) Some injustice is so awful that it's impossible to make adequate restitution, making even more remarkable that in hundreds of Bible verses, God expects us, even us, to do justice. God wouldn't have commanded it if God expected us always to fail at it.

Even though we have our problems working justice, scripture contends that God is busy creating justice out of our injustice, taking sides with the weak against the strong. Thank God that our deeds are not the only activity against injustice. Jesus said he was at work and his Father too. What we can do is be honest about our injustice, pray for forgiveness, then actively work for reconciliation and justice as our modest human attempts to witness to the work of a God who promises eventually to put things right. God's promise to judge and to work righteousness is bad news if you have benefited from injustice, good news if you have been a victim.

Though a noble goal, Christians are called to even more than doing justice. We're commanded to love.

JUSTIFICATION

Setting right. Realignment. Work that only God can do.

Jesus decisively launches God's great justification operation. On the cross, Christ somehow solves our God problem, rips open the heavens and sweeps us up into God's justifying intentions.

We figured that things between us and God were not all that bad, but when Jesus spoke to us of God, and rubbed our noses in the rags of our presumed righteousness . . . well, let's just say that we thought we were good until we met him. He called upon us to attempt great moral feats and then watched us fall flat on our faces. He invited us to join his movement and then set that kingdom's bar so high we couldn't reach it on our own. When it came time for us to stand up and show what we were made of, we slithered into the darkness. He said, "Come to me, all you who are struggling hard and carrying heavy loads." We responded in unison, "Crucify him!"

True, we were way out of line (and still are). As Paul says, all have sinned and fallen short of the glory of God, way short. All. Even in our wonderment at Christ's marvelous, painful work in our behalf, we keep getting the God/human relationship wrong. Thus, we cling to Paul's promise: "The one who started a good work in you will stay with you to complete the job." Jesus, the faithful, resourceful lover who keeps on loving those who don't know how to love him.

KINGDOM OF GOD

Realm of God. Kingdom of Heaven. Politics of Jesus.

God's realm is radically different from our dominions; otherwise Jesus would not have spent so much time attempting to explain it in his parables. When God at last gets what God wants, God's will done on earth as in heaven, God's politics come to fruition.

Jesus's miracles are irruptions of the kingdom of God; brief, inexplicable, surprising manifestations of God's intentions. In Christ, the invasion has begun, some enemy territory has been reclaimed, and God's rule is being established through a few outposts and enclaves otherwise known as church.

All the baptized are ambassadors for the coming realm, those sent out into foreign territory with the message of reconciliation and liberation: Listen up! Caesar is not in charge anymore. You're included. Get on board with God's kingdom.

Another thing: we don't get to bring in God's realm; God brings it to us as a tiny mustard seed grown up into a shrub (or a tree, depending on whether you listen to Matthew or Mark). A kingdom won through a cross, a sovereign who reigns as the bloody Lamb, an empire populated by the wretched of the earth, a seed growing silently, yeast leavening the whole lump of dough, weeds spreading uncontrollably, a dragnet cast into the sea, buried treasure: ah, to what shall we compare it?

So we pray, "Thy kingdom come." Bring it on, Lord!

LORD

An everyday term of human respect. A political title.

Early on some said, "Jesus is Lord." Christians "call on the Lord's name" in the same way Israel called upon God. The Old Testament reserved for God the title *Adonai*, Lord, but New Testament writers had no hesitancy in bestowing it upon Jesus, thus forever mixing religion and politics. Jesus is not only friend, savior, teacher, preacher; Jesus rules. He is meant not only to be loved but to be obeyed. He has not only compassion for us but also authority over us.

Jesus as Lord is Jesus recognized as considerably more than a personal opinion.

LORD'S PRAYER

What we got when we asked, "Lord, teach us to pray."

Say what you will about the defects of the disciples, in their plea for instruction, they show awareness that prayer, like just about everything "in Jesus's name," is not innate.

No way we would pray like this on our own. It takes Jesus just a few minutes to teach us his prayer, a lifetime to pray it by heart.

Pray like this:	Jesus loves his disciples enough to teach us the words for proper conversation with God.
Our	Prayer in Jesus's name is not solo. My God must be named as ours.
Father,	Address God with the same intimacy as does the Son.
who is in heaven,	The God who turned to us across a great divide enables us to address God.
uphold the holiness of your name.	Go ahead, God: be as righteous and just as you want, even if your sanctity collides with our profanity.
Bring in your kingdom	Politics! God rules, whether the potentates of the age like it or not.

so that your will is done on earth as it's done in heaven.	In heaven though God may be, God is determined to have God's way here and now with God's earth. There's no place to hide.
Your will be done.	Spoken not in resignation but as a battle cry: Lord, let there be revolution and let it begin with me.
Give us the bread we need for today.	Specific human need—that often preoccupies our prayers—is unmentioned until midway through and then only as bread enough to sustain for each day. Petition for bread is an admission that we are creatures—fragile, dependent, and contingent upon the gifts of God and the labor of others. In contrast to the "prayer list" in many congregations, physical health and wellness don't make it into the Lord's Prayer. Maybe Jesus has a different notion of our most pressing needs?
Forgive us for the ways we have wronged you,	Right after we ask for bread, Jesus insists that we plead for forgiveness for the ways we've done God wrong.
just as we also forgive those who have wronged us.	Oh my. In a prayer that asks God to do so much, now we're told the one thing that we must do: forgive—just as God forgives us—unconditionally.
And don't lead us into temptation, but rescue us from the evil one.	Life with Jesus is no cakewalk; struggle comes with the territory. Baptism is not inoculation against evil. The saved never become so secure as to not need rescue. Temptations abound; one of the greatest is the lure to make prayer into presentation of our wish list to God rather than give-and-take conversation with God.

LOVE

We thought we knew what the word love meant; then we met Jesus.

Because "I love you" can mean "I love me and want to use you to love me even more," the church links love to fidelity, urging us (in our rites of baptism and holy matrimony) to submit our declarations of love to a promise to love. Love in Christ's name is something you vow to do, an act of the will, just like God promises to love us.

Paul's famous hymn to love, 1 Corinthians 13—extolling love as greater even than faith and hope—is a favorite at weddings. Sorry, Paul wasn't a big fan of matrimony. It's a hymn to be sung by a divided congregation about the only way to get along with each other in church: a dogged determination to love and be loved among the unlovable and the unlovely in the same doggedly determined way Christ has loved the church.

Maybe that's why Jesus commanded rather than suggested love. Left up to our feelings or inclinations, would we ever love our enemies?

After Jesus told us not to break our promises to love in marriage, a man came up to Jesus asking about obtaining eternal life.

Jesus looked at him, "loved him," and said (because he loved him), "Go, sell all you have, give it to the poor, then you can be my disciple." Just about the only time Jesus is reputed to have loved an individual.

You sure you want to be loved by Jesus?

MARRIAGE

Two people making promises to love each other no matter what.

Marriage is not of major interest to Jesus except for Jesus showing up at a wedding and causing trouble by producing more wine than anybody ought to serve at a wedding reception, then prohibiting men from remarriage after divorce, and saying there's no matrimony in eternity. If you burn with lust and can't contain your beastly appetites, advised Paul, go ahead and get married. This material is not promising for a sermon on family values.

Paul offered a bit of advice for husbands and wives, though his heart wasn't in it. After extolling spousal obedience and love, Paul says he's not talking about marriage (with which he has no first-hand experience) but about the church. *Ecclesia* is Jesus responding to the world as husbands and wives respond to each other in marriage (careful using that in a sermon).

Marriage can be training in Christianity. In marriage we may discover that love isn't the cause of marriage but the fruit of having kept one's promise to another "for better or worse, for richer, for poorer, in sickness and in health," as the Service of Matrimony puts it. If you get good enough, in spite of yourself, receiving the stranger who sleeps next to you, you are better able to receive the stranger, Christ. If you can forgive your enemy—who knows the truth about you and can use it against you in a marital argument—then God may test you further by granting you children.

Marriage isn't necessary for salvation; baptism is one at a time. The church grows by witness and conversion rather than by couples having babies.

Lifelong, monogamous fidelity, which appears to be Jesus's greatest concern in marriage, requires commitment. Unsurprising that many fail at it; surprising that so many claim it's the best thing in their lives. If some nonhetero folks want into marriage, I say, let 'em have a go; the rest of us haven't done all that well.

MARY

Mother of Jesus, who bore the Son of God into the world.

Other than the Trinity, only Pontius Pilate and Mary are mentioned by name in the Apostles' Creed. Pontius Pilate said no to Jesus, Mary said yes—the two poles of human response to God. Even though Mary was warned that Jesus would be a sword through her heart, she magnified God anyway, clinch-fistedly singing that the baby in her womb would cast down the proud, send the rich away empty, and fill the poor with good things, bourgeois propriety be damned.

When a man dressed in white—not a gynecologist—appears before Mary, Mary responds, "Haven't a clue what's going on here, but nevertheless, I am willing to be part of it." Therefore, Mary is known as the very first disciple, the first to consent to be swept up in the purposes of God in Jesus Christ. Because she said yes, Mary makes possible the salvation of the world; therefore she's a model for the rest of us.

Mary was honored by the church for her docile submission to God's inscrutable will. I praise her as the first to be jolted by the promises of God and say, "I don't know where this is headed, but count me in."

MESSIAH

Christ. The anointed. Political/military leader.

After his resurrection, the disciples ask, "Lord, are you going to restore the kingdom to Israel now?" That is, "Lord, will you finally act like a messiah, mount your warhorse, raise an army, rout the Romans, and make Israel great again?"

Politics is power, our go-to means of solving the world's problems. "Jesus, when will you forgo this spirit talk for something really important—like politics?" Jesus responded by telling his followers, in effect, "I'm the messiah, but not the one you have been expecting."

Patriotism, though widely acclaimed, is not a specifically Christian virtue. If you have great reverence for government, flag in your church, respect for the military that bolsters governments, you'll find Jesus an offense to your sensibilities. The modern state—with its pronouncements, parades, propaganda, public works projects, and assorted patriotic paraphernalia—meshes uneasily with Jesus.

When asked about paying taxes to Caesar, Jesus asked for a coin (his pockets were empty), noted Caesar's image on it (sad to stamp your picture on money in order to feel good about yourself), and said, "Give it back if it means so much to him. But you be careful— never give Caesar what's God's." So what's God's? "The whole earth is the Lord's," says the psalm; not much left for the rule of Caesar. Trouble is, though God made it all and has it all, Caesar wants it all. At Jesus's birth, Herod had the good sense to be uneasy, and "all Jerusalem with him."

Jesus is very "political" but not as we desired. "So you are a king?" asked Pilate, sarcasm dripping from his urbane Roman lips. Jesus responded, "My kingdom isn't from here." Not from here with all your regal tinsel, propped up with swords. Christ's authority derives from elsewhere. A short time later, Jesus is crucified by democracy in action as the priests unanimously confess, "We have no king but the emperor."

Jesus did not, especially in Mark, embrace the title of "messiah." Peter acclaims, "You are the Christ!" Jesus tells him to keep quiet, explaining that he must suffer, be rejected, and be killed. A messiah executed as common criminal? Only when Jesus as prisoner stands before the high priest, lackey for the government, does he admit to being messiah. Now he goes head-to-head with the powers that be and, from an ignominious cross, robs them of their glory.

Jesus makes us free to be actively political and at the same time free of enthrallment to political and social reform. We wish the state well in its fumbling attempts at justice and peace and may even occasionally assist by rolling up our sleeves and working with it or by marching in the streets and shaking our fists against it, but the political vision instilled in us by a crucified messiah keeps us praying for more than even good government can give.

Best to remove that flag from the front of your church; you've got your hands full parading behind the cross.

MIRACLE

From the Latin word for wonder. The normal activity of God that, in our limited modern world view seems to us miraculous, occasional, unusual, inexplicable, and therefore an excuse for doubt.

Jesus performed wonders as a spontaneous outbreak of compassion, a sign of the advent of God's reign, a preview for what was to come. Yet few learned much from his miracles. Nobody said, "Wow. He works wonders. I'll sign up to be crucified with him."

Wonders call for wonderment rather than explanation. God is forever busy for the good of the world, but we don't always perceive that busyness or attribute the good to God. We are conditioned to ask the scientific question, "How could this happen?" rather than the theological, "Who's behind this?"

The well-heeled among us solve most of our problems with our credit cards, but there are others whose best hope is in the miraculous. If you presuppose "Miracles can't happen," you won't find any in scripture or anywhere else. A world governed by natural law— safely sealed shut from incursions, cause-effect explained—gets edgy when Christ's miracles disrupt the truce that science has made with the inexplicable.

Miracles comprise those events that lead us to delightful recognition that creation continues, that reality is not as fixed and final as we've been led to believe. Rarely do we fully understand what's going on, and yet we have a sense that a door has opened, the curtain pulled back, and for just one wondering moment, we see.

We pray for miraculous intervention in times of sickness or difficulty because, now that we know God's benevolent intentions for us in Jesus Christ, we are justified in believing that God wills our good and strives with us against evil. Praying to God to work wonders is okay as long as we say as Jesus did, "However, not my will but your will must be done."

John calls miracles "signs." Jesus's very first "sign" occurred not in a church service, not out of compassion for a crippled person, but at a bash after a wedding when Jesus, without saying a word or waving a magic wand, turned 180 gallons of water into fine wine, just to show he could do it. Seeing the sign, his disciples "believed in him," though who knows what they believed; they had not yet heard him teach or preach. Water to wine, enough bread to feed a hungry multitude, the blind see, the lame walk, Lazarus breathes again, the poor hear good news preached—signs pointing to a wonderful possibility. Something's afoot.

MISSION

God's sending.

Christianity, like the Trinity, is by nature centrifugal, extroverted. Even as the Father sends the Son and the Father and Son send the Holy Spirit in order that humanity can be sent back to the Father and Son, so Christ sends us. Called to Christ, we are sent from Christ who looks upon every corner of the world and declares, "Mine!"

Jesus calls himself the "light of the world," then sends us missionaries to share his light, thus fulfilling the prophet's promise: "I will also appoint you as light to the nations, so that my salvation may reach to the end of the earth." How? "You will be my witnesses in Jerusalem, in all Judea and Samaria, and to the end of the earth." How? "Whenever you enter a city and its people welcome you, eat what they set before you. Heal the sick who are there, and say to them, 'God's kingdom has come upon you.'"

Mission is God's grace in action, the gospel taken over a human boundary, Christ received from the hands of another. The Christian life is schooling in gratitude that "salvation is from the Jews." Every congregation began as some church's mission. No congregation is yet "church" if it's not planting another. Someone had to love Jesus and you enough to be a missionary to you.

American Christians are waking up to a post-Christian culture, missionaries to the world that we thought we owned. Pastors are better than a congregation's unctuous ambulance chasers. The pastor is lead missionary. The congregation equips missionaries to join Christ in giving away to the world the news it can't come up with on its own. In our time the American church has the opportunity to reawake to the wonder of Jews coming even unto us Gentiles, telling us the news that we're included.

Discipleship is first training in receptivity, receiving good news from the hands of another, and second is joining Christ in his mission as those who know are commanded to show and tell those who don't yet know.

A shrinking congregation is probably one where the boundaries of God's kingdom were constricted. Parochial. Members got confused into thinking that the church is the private clinic where their aches and pains are assuaged rather than a field hospital where those who've been wounded in service to Christ's mission are bandaged up and sent back into the fray.

"As the Father has sent me," Jesus says, "so I send you."

NEIGHBOR

Anybody for whom you are given responsibility by Jesus.

"Who is my neighbor that I'm to love as much as I love myself?" a lawyer asked Jesus. Jesus responded with an unforgettable parable. Neighbor is not the nice folks in church who are, after all, a lot like you. Neighbor is a stranger dying in the ditch whom Jesus forces you to help without resenting the neighbor for not being like you. Neighbor is also a Samaritan, whom you despise, who also is your salvation when you're down and dying, the one who knows God differently from the way you know God but who serves God better than you.

The story wouldn't be challenging if Jesus urged us to love humanity in general. Anybody can do that. We are to love the neighbor, the one upstairs who plays loud rock music after midnight even though you have politely asked him not to, and who, the next morning, is the only person who offers to help you start your pick-up so you can get to work.

Neighbor love is only one of the ways that Jesus makes impossible for his followers to live normal lives.

OMNI

All. Omnipotent, omniscient, omnipresent.

Whenever affixed to another word, be warned: you are probably about to be sold a nonbiblical abstraction, such that God is generalized, large, distant, vague, and controlling. As a pandemic robs us of our faith that we've got the whole world in our hands, we are drawn to the notion that somewhere up there, out there, there's an all-encompassing, impersonal force that's in control of everything, knows everything, and is in everything. Christians believe that though God could be all-powerful, God chose to be love personified rather than abstract, Jesus Christ, returning the world to God.

ONAN

Too much information.

Ordered by God to impregnate his widowed sister-in-law (in order to give the bereft woman a family and a future), Onan refused and "wasted his semen on the ground." For this, God killed Onan, thus forever casting a shadow over coitus interruptus and instilling fear into the hearts of adolescent boys.

While the Bible includes everything we need to know for our salvation, you got to love the Bible for including much that we'll never, ever need to know.

PARABLE

Small story with big point.

Jesus's preaching is distinguished by his parables—pithy, deceptively simple stories drawn from everyday life that subvert everyday life. If you must have your revelation immediately practical, obvious, and straightforward, go worship obviousness and practicality rather than parabolist Jesus.

On the other hand, if you delight in being teased, cajoled, surprised, jolted, there's nobody better than Jesus when he's on a roll with his stories.

"Tell us who God is," we asked. "You're not the God we craved or expected." Jesus replied not with a three-point lecture but with a sermonic short story: "A farmer went forth to scatter seed . . ." The sower carefully, meticulously preparing the ground, removing rocks and weeds, one furrow six inches from another. . . .

No! This farmer just slings seed.

A dragnet full of sea creatures is hauled into the boat. Sort the catch, separating good from bad? No. The fisherman cares more for the size of the haul than the quality of the catch.

A field is planted. But when the seed germinates, weeds grow alongside the wheat. "An enemy has done this!" cries the farmer. Enemy, my foot. This is the agricultural mess you get when you so carelessly sling seed.

Cull the wheat from the weeds? "No, good plants or bad, I just love to see things grow," says the casual farmer.

While plowing, a farmhand's plow hits something hard. Buried treasure! He covers it up with soil, sells all that he has, and goes to the owner of the field saying, "Call me crazy, but how much would you take for that worthless patch of dirt?"

Which of you, having lost a sheep, will not abandon the ninety-nine (who lack the creativity to roam), leaving them to fend for themselves in the wilderness, and beat the bushes until you find the one lost? When at last you find the sheep, which of you will not rush home and call to your friends, "Let's party! My sheep that was lost is found!"

"While you were wasting time looking for that one," your neighbors reply, "your flock dwindled by two-thirds."

Which of you, journeying down the Jericho road, upon seeing a perfect stranger lying in the ditch half-dead and bleeding, would not risk your life, put the injured man on the leather seats of your Jaguar, take him to the hospital, max out your credit cards in his recovery, and more?

None of us would behave so unseemly, recklessly, and extravagantly.

These are not stories about us. They are stories of God. We, who have been malformed into thinking that church is where we learn who we are and what we're supposed to do, who ask of every story, "What's in this for me?" must be coaxed, teased, lured, dislodged from our presumption that we already know all about God. Therefore, parables.

Mark and Matthew say that Jesus said nothing except in parables, which seems an exaggeration until we realize that Jesus was a parable: the storyteller become the story teasing us toward God.

PASTOR

Judean businessperson. Eventually a name for Christian leaders.

It's tough for pastors to help Jesus without getting in his way. Pastors are middle managers who care for the flock so that it may join Jesus in caring for the world. A pastor can't be hired; a pastor must be called, sent, that is, coerced by God to serve God's people as they serve God.

Because a pastor's care for the flock is in the name of Jesus, pastoral care is more than mere hand-holding and ruffled feathers soothing. It's vocational care that patches up laity who have been damaged while working with Jesus so that they can be sent back to the frontlines where the battle rages.

"Pastor" is not a name for a "preacher" without teeth, a quivering mass of availability who substitutes popularity and a pleasing personality for honesty and truth telling. A pastor is someone who in imitation of Psalm 23 leads the flock by still waters and into green pastures so that the often-wayward sheep may be in good shape for the world's shearing and slaughter.

PAUL

First-century Jewish leader-scholar who was impressed into service by the risen Christ as church planter and missionary to the pagans.

Paul is known to us mostly through his letters, our earliest documentation of Jesus as one with the God of Israel. The eighteenth-century notion that Paul took the simple teaching of a rural rabbi and made it all complicated and theological is sentimental bosh. The presence of the risen Christ determined how deep Paul's thinking had to dive, to what theological heights Paul had to climb to figure out the implications of the astounding reality that God was in Christ reconciling the whole world to himself.

Likewise the Reformation idea that Pharisee Paul rejected his Judaism because it was too constricting, demanding, and legalistic isn't fair to Paul's theology. Paul dared to question Torah, not because it was legalistic but because it wasn't Christ. In Christ, Paul saw that the God of Torah had graciously, surprisingly, personally expanded and enabled what God had done for Israel to reach even as far as the Gentiles.

At a time when the church was fighting for its life, Paul presents Christ in all of Christ's present, cosmic, universal, daily relevant glory, pulling out some major theological artillery,

1. To enable the first Christians to stay focused on the wonder of God's beneficence in Christ, and

2. To keep squabbling Christians together in the church.

Throughout most of the church's life, we've been unable to keep up with Paul. Any grand reclamation of the church's witness has usually required a rediscovery of Paul's discoveries, particularly as dazzlingly displayed in his Letter to the Romans.

Like any of us preachers, Paul said some cringeworthy things (about women, marriage, enslavement) that contradict his core theological affirmations. Fortunately, Paul's gospel makes up for Paul's bad-sermon-days.

PEACE

Shalom; God's peace means more than absence of war.

Jesus was prince of peace, but not as the world thinks of peace. Christ brings a peace that passes understanding.

Much that passes for peace is only a temporary truce with the truth. "I'm at peace" means "I've given up worrying about what's true; contentment is all I can handle." A congregation that's unified and at peace with itself is often a church that's tired of trying to be church and now is a club for like-minded older adults.

Jesus warned us that his peace is not peace, but a sword. He renders our placid existence profoundly unsafe by leaving us with his peace that made no peace with a world at war against his truth. Once God turned to us and chose us to be for God, we haven't had a moment's peace.

PELAGIAN

We are well-intentioned good people who are making progress.

Once Christianity became respectable, after Constantine, lots of people got baptized, living out their baptisms with varying degrees of seriousness (just like today). British monk Pelagius, contemporary of Augustine, abhorred this moral laxity, saying that once you become a Christian, it's your job to lead a holy life in which you cease to sin.

Augustine countered that's a naive, even arrogant undertaking. We are not good enough to choose our way into goodness. Any good that we do is always a gift of God's grace working in us, often in spite of us; good intentions alone are inadequate to lead us to do good. Our sin is so deeply rooted in our thinking and willing that our only hope is for God's grace to do for us what we cannot do for ourselves. "Not I, but Christ in me," said Paul.

We have the capacity to choose rightly, therefore, we must, countered the Pelagians. Our relationship with God is up to us and our good decisions and deeds.

Pelagius lost the argument to Augustine in North Africa yet won among Christians in North America. A cardinal principle of American Christianity is that we are basically nice people headed in the right direction and, despite occasional setbacks, we're doing the best we can. "I try to live a good life and do good unto others, and after all, isn't that what Christianity is all about?" Church is where we come for a weekly moral boost. Preaching is when we get our assignment for the week. Rather than being good news of what God has done, faith becomes self-confidence that you've got the right stuff to hoist yourself up to God. Christianity reduced to another technique for self-improvement. Autosalvation. Do this, do that, and you will ascend to being as fine a person as you know yourself to be. Little wonder that fatigue sets in.

Orthodox Christianity, tutored by Augustine, has said otherwise. God has predestined God's self to be our God. We are not loved because we are loveable; we love because we are loved. Any goodness we achieve is responsive. We who are so addicted to self-love are actually capable of love because we have been loved. It is possible, even for people like us, to do and be good because God got ahold of us and will never, ever let us go.

Now, go be as good as God means you to be.

PRAYER

Conversation with the God who initiates, yearns for, and sustains conversation with us.

Connectivity with God comes easily, naturally, only for Jesus. As Paul says, "We don't know how to pray." "Teach us to pray" is one of the few times the disciples asked for instruction. In response, Jesus gave a model prayer: "When you pray," say these words.

The most important thing in prayer according to Jesus is dogged persistence, not because God needs our nagging but because we need to keep learning how to be in conversation with a true, living God who responds not always as we ask, but as God knows we need. We're not just talking to ourselves. Any friendship takes time for all the necessary colloquies. In any good conversation, there is honest speaking and courageous listening, pregnant pauses and knowing silences, and thereby the possibility that we may end the conversation different from the way we began.

To make room in our cluttered lives for the romping of the Holy Spirit—to focus amid our distraction upon what God cares about—is to put ourselves at God's disposal. Thus, in one way or another, every prayer "in Jesus's name" concludes as Jesus ended his most fierce conversation with his Father, "Nevertheless, not my will but thine be done." Don't pray if you are unwilling for your prayer to be answered, as Jesus's prayer was in Gethsemane, "No."

Persist. Go ahead and knock. The door will be opened just a bit more, though not always leading into a place you expected. Sometimes what seems to us as unanswered prayer is an unexpected answer. What sounded like no was God giving us not what we thought we just had to have, but what we had no idea we needed.

Prayer is the risky willingness to participate in God's freedom to curse and to bless, to kill and to make alive, to open and shut, to pluck and to plant, and all in God's own good time. We're not informing God of what God doesn't know. Rather, in prayer, God gives us a part to play in God's work in the world. God invites us to join in God's redemptive, reconciling, healing activity. As Christ constantly intercedes for us in the power of the Holy Spirit, our times of prayer enable us to join the Father-Son-Holy Spirit colloquy. The prayer that began, "Lord, help me," ends with, "Lord, enable me to help you. Put me in the game; give me the ball."

Maybe our problem with prayer is not that our expectations are outlandish but that our intercession is paltry. We pray for personal healing or happiness when Jesus taught us first to pray, "Thy kingdom come, thy will be done." We beseech benevolence for friends and family; Jesus commanded prayer for enemies and persecutors.

Because prayer is as life-giving as breathing, it's good to set aside specific times of the day to pray, to get into the rhythm of inhaling and exhaling with the Holy Spirit. Since prayer is more than just spilling your guts, it's helpful to be guided by the saints, allowing them to feed us the words, praying through the words that have bolstered God's people for two thousand years. Left to my own devices, without prompting from a prayer book, fat chance that I would pray for the president, the governor, and others in authority over me.

It's a good idea, while listening to God, to listen to ourselves. As in the art of conversation, we can get better at prayer over time. While we attempt to inform God, God often transforms us; as we're letting God know what God needs to do, God reveals to us what God needs doing. We thought we were turning to God in prayer only to have God turn to us. Or as Paul put it, sometimes giving us words, sometimes with sighs too deep for words the Holy Spirit helps us to pray.

PREACHING

Speaking up and speaking out for God by speaking with God.

The gospel is a living word, spoken before it is written. Through the ages we asked, "Is God really with us or not?" In response, God comes alongside as Word made flesh, preacher John the Baptist precursor to John's cousin, Jesus, the paradigmatic preacher.

"Now after John was arrested [preachers take note], Jesus came to Galilee, announcing God's good news, saying, 'Time's up! Here comes God's kingdom! Change your hearts and lives, and trust this good news!'"

Emmanuel's occupation? Preaching. Luke says Jesus's first apocalyptic assault upon the world-as-it-is was from a synagogue pulpit, quoting his favorite preacher, "The Spirit of the Lord is upon me . . . to preach good news." He announces a revolution, world change initiated by nothing but words. Though the Nazareth congregation responded to his sermon with "Let's kill him," Jesus kept preaching. Still does.

A preacher's main challenges are:

1. Preaching is first about God, what God wants to talk about and how God wants to say it, and only second-arily, if there's time, is preaching about us. As Paul said, "We don't preach about ourselves."

2. The burden of Jesus's brash, "Whoever listens to you, listens to me."

The Word of God comes from God, through the lips of thoroughly human (and, if you know us personally, very flawed) preachers, to God's (faulty, contentious, obdurate, truth-resistant) people. Preaching is the typical performance one might expect from preacher

Jesus, fully God and fully human, God making human words God's word, God refusing to be silent, God insisting on having the last word, God refusing to be God alone.

Jesus told a story of a crazy farmer who—without carefully preparing good, receptive soil—just started slinging seed. Most of the seed was wasted, gobbled up by birds, choked by weeds. A few seeds germinated and bore fruit. This farming failure Jesus calls a miraculous harvest.

Preachers love that parable.

Preaching is not difficult because listeners are inattentive, truth averse, and dull (ah, the average congregation!) but due to Christ, the Word we didn't expect from God. Preachers have the daunting task of standing before a church and saying, "Listen up! Here's truth that you have spent all week avoiding."

Still, faith comes from hearing. The Christian faith is acoustically produced, auditory, God daring to entrust "the message of reconciliation" to frail envoys. Preachers keep preaching, God keeps speaking through sermons, and people keep hearing anyhow.

Though failure is expected, our job as preachers is to sling the seed; the harvest is up to God. Preachers don't work alone. It's not a sermon until the Holy Spirit shows up, rips a sermon out of my hands, makes a dull religious lecture into pyrotechnic proclamation, and enables my words to romp through the hapless congregation as God's address to them. If anybody hears anything from a sermon of mine, it's a miracle.

In spite of all the reasons why people neither listen to nor get much out of sermons, the prophet promises that God's word "shall not return empty." Evidence for that bold claim? You are reading this book.

PRELAPSARIAN

Before the fall. You will never need this word, but sometimes throwing "prelapsarian" into a conversation can impress your friends.

There's them that believes that God became incarnate as the Christ in order to solve the problem of our lapse into sin—God's plan B for human salvation after God's plan A went haywire in the garden. Postlapsarians.

Prelapsarians say that Jesus is more than the solution for our fallen sinfulness; Christ was always who God is and what God is up to all along. God didn't wait until the incarnation in order to be God for us. From all eternity—even before creation—God is Father, Son, and Holy Spirit resolute to be in relationship with us creatures. In his incarnation, Christ is the eternal, ebullient overflowing of God's love into all of God's creation. God doing something about our sin, yes, but more—God always the God turned toward us.

PRODIGAL SON

If you know nothing of Jesus, there's a good chance you know one of Jesus's greatest hits: the parable of the prodigal son.

The parable appeals to those who have been either

1. the wild younger kid who abandons the old man only to hit bottom, come to your senses, remember who you are, return and rediscover your father running to welcome you with a party, or

2. the respectable, responsible (and eventually resentful) older sibling who stayed home and shouldered more than your share of the responsibility only to have Dad gallingly welcome back your wayward brat of a brother

with the biggest bash this hick town has ever seen and
then have the nerve to beg you to come in, get down,
and party.

In other words, the parable of the prodigal son is beloved as
a story about some of us all of the time and most of us some of
the time.

That's fine, as long as you remember that the most interestingly
reckless character in the story is not the bad-boy younger brother
or the stuffy homebody, older sibling. The most interesting actor is
the Father who gives, waits, receives, gives, and pleads. The prodigal
comes to his senses and turns back home to the Father's extravagant,
raucous welcome. The older brother must endure the Father leaving
the party and coming out into the darkness to plead with him to
join the celebration saying, "All that I have is yours!" Finally, both
siblings, even in their differences, must deal with the Father's love
for both.

Did the younger gratefully straighten up his life and fly right?
Did the older ever loosen up and let down his moral pretentions
and get down and party? Jesus doesn't say. I doubt they lived happily
ever after.

PROGRESS

"Look at us: onward and upward we go."

The Bible does eschatology, never progress. Americans enjoy
thinking that we are making progress. Leaving behind ignorance and
error, we have at last progressed to where we can stand on our own
two feet and view the world unconstrained by the mistakes and er-
rors of our ancestors. The Bible is so old, the Jews are so primitive
and violent; we have solved so many mysteries and improved the

world so much, thought so deeply, progressed so far; what have these Old Testament Jews to do with us?

Election of a bankrupt casino owner as president? COVID-19 killing Americans of color more than people who look like me? Mere slight downward detours in our upward ascent. Look at us.

While we thought we were progressively expanding our world view, our vision didn't grow; it shrunk. In arriving ten minutes before the discovery of truth, we were two thousand years late. We haven't gone beyond or risen above the primitive credulity of our forebears; truth to tell, we have never been able to keep up with Jesus.

PROPHETS

God-obsessed preachers, poets, brassy evangelists, and disrespectful rabble rousers personally chosen by God, to give Israel the bad news of coming exile, sustain through the horrors of Babylonian captivity, announce homecoming, then direct reconstitution as God's Torah-loving covenant people—with nothing but words.

The prophets dared, even in their full, flawed humanity, unabashedly to preach, "Thus says the Lord," making it hard to tell if it's God talking or Isaiah.

Most prophets, like Moses, had enough sense to know that they didn't want to be prophets. Jeremiah's call is paradigmatic:

The Lord says, "Before I created you in the womb I knew you; before you were born I set you apart; I made you a prophet to the nations."

Jeremiah begs off: "Ah, Lord God, I don't know how to speak because I'm only a child."

The Lord's response? "Don't say, 'I'm only a child.' Where I send you, you must go; what I tell you, you must say. Don't be afraid of them, because I'm with you to rescue you."

Then the Lord says, "I'm putting my words in your mouth. This very day I appoint you over nations and empires, to dig up and pull down, to destroy and demolish, to build and plant."

Quite a preaching future for a fetus. Old worlds deconstructed, dismantled; new worlds formed, reformed, with some of the pushiest, poetic, plucky speech ever. Prophets preach poetry—plucking and planting, bowl of fruit, valley of dry bones, smashing pots, locusts, fire, and a plumb line. God works on Israel nonviolently with words put to the lips of preachers.

Please note that God's word comes to, rather than from, prophets: "I consecrated you; I appointed . . . you shall speak whatever I command. . . . I am with you. . . . I have put words in your mouth." Thus Amos speaks, not because he has something he needs to get off his chest, but rather because God has something to say: "A lion roars; who will not fear? The Lord God has spoken; who can but prophesy?" Beaten up by the rigors of the preaching life, Jeremiah resolves not to speak again about God, but then there's a burning in his belly: "I'm drained trying to contain it; I'm unable to do it." Ezekiel hears God say, "I've made you a lookout for the house of Israel. When you hear a word from me, deliver my warning."

Prophets are distinguished by their lack of originality; they never get to preach what they personally might like to say. Delivering the words of God often lands prophets in political hot water. Amos was told by court chaplain Amaziah, "Never again prophesy at Bethel, for it is the king's holy place and his royal house." Unlike court chaplains, White House clergy sycophants, or deans of university chapels who play safe by saying what the regime wants to hear, prophets preach what God wants said.

When challenged, Amos blamed his preaching upon the Lord: "I am not a prophet, nor am I a prophet's son; I am a shepherd, and a trimmer of sycamore trees. But the Lord took me from shepherding the flock, and the Lord said to me, 'Go, prophesy to my people Israel.'"

When the congregation whines about something ill said in a sermon, preachers discover powerful freedom in being able to retort, "Though I'm no Amos, Jeremiah or Hosea, just like them, being a preacher wasn't my idea of a good time. I preach what I've been told to preach. Got a problem with my sermon? Take it up with the Lord."

PROVIDENCE

Capital of Rhode Island. Our assurance that, though we can't always see God at work in the world or in us, God provides.

Providence is best known in the backward view, a matter of faith, hope, and love not seen at the time. Looking back upon your life, said Augustine, it's as if you are gazing into a chicken pen with random chicken tracks in the mud. But then, if you look through the eyes of faith, you begin to discern pattern, direction, presence, and beneficence that were there all along.

God can ride a lame horse or shoot with a crooked bow. A redemptive God is not stumped by our screw-ups or by the way the world tries to screw us up. Though God doesn't will suffering, God can use even pain to lure us closer. Thus, amid life's twists and turns, the Christian says, "It will be interesting to see what God makes of this."

"God is in control" is what's left of the idea of providence. God could have been in control, instead, God chose to be in love. "Loving" and "controlling," two words that rarely go together. God doesn't always get God's way in the present moment; not everything that happens occurs because God wills it. Even though God knows us so well that God knows what we'll do, God has chosen to create us as those who are free to do as we damn well please.

Better than saying, "God has a plan for my life," is to believe that ultimately, when all is said and done (though I may not be able to see it now), God is able to pick up the pieces of the mess I've made. Nothing will defeat the purposes of God. God's chief end? To love, to connect now so that, by love rather than coercion, we may be turned toward God eternally.

Providence is God refusing to allow us to determine the ultimate goal and meaning of our story. Our sin and stupidity don't control how it finally is between us and God. A providential God loves to commandeer our stories, or, subtly, occasionally dramatically, sometimes steadily moving and, sometimes awkwardly jerking the course of our history, but always making our story God's.

QUIETISM

Passive inwardness and resignation. Refusal of the agency God has given me to be part of God's work in the world. Spiritual sloth.

Realizing that my relationship with God is God's self-assignment, I come to believe that I should do nothing for God, failing to respond to the God who has turned toward me and bragging about it as a sign of my spiritual humility. Condemned by Pope Innocent XI and John Wesley, who said, in different ways, that a beloved who fails to return love has misunderstood love.

RACISM

The modern sin of designating people by their physical characteristics to oppress and demean them. A perversion of the Christian faith. The church egregiously capitulating to and legitimating European colonization.

White racism has got to be the greatest infidelity of the North American church. Sporting events, schools, and even bars are more racially inclusive than the UMC. Exclusion on the basis of race is illegal everywhere but church; there, we are free to congregate with whom we choose.

At its most effective, baptism washes away the superficial, sinful distinctions that we impose upon one another. Our racialized church is judgment upon us white Christians, an indication of how far we've got to go before we live as if "one Lord, one faith, one baptism" were true.

White racial sin is a grand opportunity for white Christians to show that Christ enables us to:

1. Be born again in a culture that acts as if we are stuck repeating our parents' sins.
2. Tell the truth about the sin of our whiteness.

REALISM

Trying to convince Christians to do something Jesus wouldn't.

"I didn't vote for him to be pastor-in-chief. He's commander-in-chief. Besides, Lincoln lied too."

"Christ is a noble ideal, but sometimes we must face facts. Christians, get real."

"Jesus's ethics are fine for individuals but are irrelevant and unrealistic for social and governmental matters."

Such talk begs the question, "Who gets to define reality?"

Natural among us is a desperation for normality, placidity, and order: the sweet narcotic of the status quo. The present regime, whether of the right or the left, works this craving to its advantage, telling us that the world as it is, is all there is. The systems in place have divine authorization. American constitutional democracy is the best of all possible worlds. The prudent adjust to, rather than rage against the machine. With a bit of level-headed tinkering, you can retrofit Jesus so that he won't make you uncomfortable.

Reality is Jesus Christ rather than official, governmentally subsidized descriptions of what's what. Somehow, Christians must love the world without trusting it.

When told that we ought to lay aside the adventurous way of Christ and "get real," Christians suspect that we are about to be sold some stripped-down version of reality. Nothing wrong with "Christian realism," except it is unchristian and unreal.

God doesn't allow us to choose our reality. Once Jesus Christ strode out of his tomb on Easter, we've never been able to make up our minds about the boundaries between what's realistically possible and what's totally improbable. Jesus didn't end his Sermon on the Mount with, "Just kidding."

"Say something practical, workable, and rational," says the world.

To which Christians reply, "Jesus Christ."

"Suggest a realistic political alternative to capitalist, free market democracy."

"Church."

RECONCILIATION

What God's up to.

Reconciliation to God is what we are meant for. In the Christ always turned toward the Father, the Father by the Holy Spirit graciously turned toward us.

We don't get to decide, on our own, whether or not we'll be in relationship with God. Nothing about us is on our own. God has made the world to be moving toward reconciliation. The grand diversity of the created world is being drawn together, God's harmony overcoming our division and exclusion.

There's so much disunion and separation among us because there's no reconciliation without truth-telling and truth-receiving. Jesus was not crucified for saying, "God loves you" but for saying, in effect, "God loves you . . . enough to tell you the truth about God, you, and your neighbor."

Many responded, "Don't bother, I'm doing fine all by myself."

Those on their way to being reconciled said, "Tell me more."

Knowing God's ultimate reconciling intentions for the world encourages followers of Jesus to get on board with God as reconcilers. (See *Atonement*.)

REPENTANCE

Wising up. Turning to the God who, in Christ, has turned to you—to change your heart and life.

Metanoia (Greek for repentance) is cousin of metamorphosis. When John the Baptist prepared the way for Christ, he told the crowds to hear the good news, get washed up, be drowned, give away surplus clothing, practice justice, in short, "Repent!"

Although Jesus discourages us from showing off our goodness, he commends public admission (confession) of badness. Critics attempted to trap Jesus in a discussion of tragedy by asking, "Hear about the tower that fell and killed those people in Siloam [natural evil] or the Galileans whom Herod executed [human evil]? What did they do to deserve that?"

Jesus responded with a non sequitur: "Unless you change your hearts and lives, you will die just as they did." If we can't repent of our temptation to keep God at a distance with our detached theological discussions of others' pain and injustice (and maybe even our books on Christian vocabulary), we'll never know much about God.

Repentance is turning and facing in a different direction whereby we are enabled to see. Until we stand under the gospel, we can't understand it. Faith is best known from the inside looking out. Salvation is free and very costly. Jesus transforms, jolts, and disorders for the better every life he touches. When God turns toward you, and you turn toward God, your life turns around.

RESURRECTION

More intimidating than a dead prophet, social activist, or teacher; Jesus is alive, present, and promises that, because of him and his work, we'll be eternally present with God too.

The women come to the cemetery in the darkness (where were the male disciples?). Jesus's tomb is empty! They run back to tell the cowering men, "He is risen! The story of Jesus and us isn't over; it's just beginning! Everything's up for grabs."

Response of the disciples? "You're nuts."

None of the disciples expected the resurrection of the crucified Jesus. Even when resurrected Christ stood before them and led the

Bible study, they couldn't see. The postresurrection appearances of Jesus are mixed with fear, misapprehension, evening meals, locked doors, breakfast on the beach, and the disciples' sexist unwillingness to believe the testimony of women. Even with the risen Christ standing in front of them speaking, some doubted. Mary Magdalene mistook him for a gardener.

God's new age breaking in among us is so new and unexpected that we have trouble bringing it to speech. The discrepancies in the Gospel accounts of Easter are testimony to Easter's reality. The resurrection is a miraculous work of God that is humanly inconceivable. Our trouble thinking about Easter doesn't mean it's untrue.

Better than a resuscitation of a dead body, the resurrection is a vindication of crucified Jesus. Much more than the return of the robin in the spring, the butterfly emerging from the cocoon, or Jesus living on in the disciples' memories, Resurrection is God's great "No!" to the forces of sin and death that nailed Jesus to the cross. The one who forgave his crucifiers, who reached out to sinner and outcast, who stood up to the authorities, and spoke of a world shifting on its axis, the one who invited everybody to jump on board his revolution and was brutally nailed to a cross, that one is the only one God ever raised from the dead.

Easter is God's victory, God's grand self-attestation as if to say, "You want to know who I am, where I'm headed, look to the only one I ever raised from the dead." Once you lay aside your prejudices and dare to believe the women running from the tomb, so much about Jesus falls into place. On the other hand, if Jesus has not been resurrected, nothing that the church or scripture claims about Christ makes sense.

No resurrected Christ, no hope. In his resurrection appearances we learned, It ain't over between us and God until God says it's over. Because of resurrection, Christians don't do dejection: "People don't change." "It's over and finished." "Get real." "Nothing to be done." If God can raise crucified Jesus, never again can we be sure what's impossible. Jesus is alive and busy, our labors are not the sole effort, and death never gets the last word.

A resurrected God keeps insisting on bringing something fresh into every situation, even the worst. The God of the exodus and the homecoming after Israel's exile loves to surprise.

It is "scary to fall into the hands of the living God." Presumably, it's not frightening to be in the hands of a dead God, a dumb idol who never surprises or demands anything, a fake, a projection of our fondest desires and silliest wishes. No wonder that the predominant Easter emotion is fear.

What's the first thing done by the risen Christ? He goes looking for his dim-witted disciples, returning to the same knuckleheads who betrayed and disappointed him. One would think that on the first day of your resurrected life you would burst into the palace in Jerusalem saying, "Pilate. You made a big mistake. Now it's payback time."

No, the risen Christ returns to Galilee, land of origin of his disciples. They didn't go looking for him; once again, he turns to them and then turned them out into the whole world.

We have never known how to take the risen Christ's words, "I am with you always." Promise or threat? It's as if Christ says, "I had but a few years to harass you before I was murdered. After resurrection, I am with you always. You'll never be able to get God off your back."

The Easter mandate? "Go! Tell somebody!"

REVELATION

God's self-disclosure. The Trinity's gracious unveiling.

Knowledge of God is not self-derived. Christianity is a revealed religion. It comes to us, not we to it, gift, all the way down. Because God is epiphanic, we don't have to guess who God is, or make up God as we go.

Revelation is what we get with a God who is relentlessly intent on turning toward us. The Father is revealer, the Son the revelation, the Spirit the revealing. Jesus is as much of God as we hope to see, God holding nothing back: "I am the way, the truth, and the life. No one comes to the Father except through me. If you have really known me, you will also know the Father. From now on you know him and have seen him."

No mere prophet talking about God or messenger from God, Jesus is a brown-skinned Jew on whose body "the fullness of God was pleased to live . . . and he reconciled all things to himself through him—whether things on earth or in the heavens. He brought peace through the blood of his cross."

Jesus doesn't just tell us the truth or merely point us toward the truth: "I am the truth." Truth not as an idea; truth is personal, a crucified Jew from Nazareth who, even when we tried to shut him up, returned and resumed the conversation. God doesn't wait for us to discover truth; God discovers us, in spite of how cleverly we have camouflaged, showing up as truth who speaks, calling us to come out of hiding and join up with the truth. Revelation is not a roadmap but a relationship.

Eventually, we won't be so empty-handed when it comes to knowledge of God. We'll say to each other, "Look! God's dwelling is here with humankind." God will dwell with us and we with God. Knowledge of God will cover the earth as abundantly as waters cover the sea.

RICHES

Considered by the world a sign of divine blessing, hard work, personal achievement, or shrewd behavior; for Jesus, dangerous, self-deluding, and an impediment to salvation.

Of all the people Jesus calls to "Follow me!" only one refused. His rebuff was due to money. "It's hard to save rich people," sighs Jesus as the well-heeled man walks away.

"How hard is it, Jesus?" asked the disciples.

"As difficult as to shove a fully loaded dromedary through the eye of a needle," he replied with a smirk.

"Still," muses Jesus, "with God even something so far-fetched as the salvation of the rich is . . . possible."

"There was a rich man whose profits exceeded his most optimistic projections. 'Soul, you've got it made,' he said to himself. That very night his life (the one thing he couldn't own) was taken. Most folks would call this man prudent and productive. God's angel addressed him as 'Fool.'"

"Hear the one about the nameless rich man who had a great life within his gated community and a poor man named Lazarus who had nothing but misery? Well, they both died (death, the one thing shared by rich and poor). The rich man, of course, went straight to hell, the poor man to the blessed bosom of Father Abraham. The rich man cries out, 'Please Father Abraham, send Lazarus to warn my wealthy brothers about their fate!' (The rich man spent much of his life sending people to do his bidding.)

"'They wouldn't listen,' scoffs Abraham. 'God's prophets had no effect on their economics. They wouldn't wise up even if somebody came back from the dead to warn them.'"

Ironically, the one who told these stories came back from the dead to tell us the truth about the fate of the rich. Some, not many, but enough to keep economists nervous, were simple enough to believe what the one come back from the dead said. They divested and hit the road with Jesus.

Said Jesus's first disciples, "Lord, we've left everything to follow you." Making all latter-day disciples in my income bracket uneasy.

Though it may be possible for God to shove a camel through the eye of a needle, it could be rough on the camel.

SABBATH

Taking time off from the gift of daily work in order to enjoy the gift of being with God.

The Sabbath command is less concerned that you take time off from your busy life than that you not allow anybody else—"sons or daughters, male or female servants, animals, and immigrants"—to labor in your behalf. Sabbath rest is your gift to your neighbor, not an ancient way to lower your blood pressure.

Obedience to the command to keep Sabbath was one of the ways that Israel was identified and preserved as God's distinctive people down through centuries of Gentile cruelty and persecution. This makes all the more remarkable that Jesus was a notorious violator of the fourth commandment, noted more for his socializing and public performances on the Sabbath than for his quiet sabbatical solitude.

Like all gifts of God, Sabbath rest can be distorted. Although it's good, amid the capitalist, acquisitive grind, to unplug, disengage, and intentionally take time off in order to hang out with God, Sabbath keeping does not deny that work can be a gift of God or that the forced solitude of the unemployed is no blessing.

A pastor's work is no more stressful and anxiety-producing than any other Christian's and therefore no more deserving of a sabbatical.

Because God never naps, the world is not on our shoulders. We can keep Sabbath knowing that God doesn't.

When Jesus was criticized for not keeping Sabbath, he responded that no work ought to be done on the Sabbath—except good work that benefits humanity.

SACRAMENTS

In a faith full of words, Christ (known for his preaching) in the sacraments shows rather than tells. An incarnated God turns to us by making the material be spiritual.

Never forgetting that we are creatures, the creator loves us as the animals we are. Not all know for sure what "love of God" signifies; everybody knows what a meal means. The Eucharist (Lord's Supper, Mass, Holy Communion) is a meal where Jesus is the host, everybody is invited, there's enough for all, and Jesus foots the bill. Who knows what "repent of your sins" means, but everybody knows what it's like to take a bath. If you've ever been honest-to-God hungry, so thirsty you thought you would die, or badly in need of a bath, you're ready to receive the sacraments.

When we give thanks for the bread and wine on Jesus's table, we're not saying that this food is unholy until the priest zaps it with religious words and makes it holy. All bread is holy as gift of God and human labor. Trouble is, at breakfast it's hard to appreciate bread's sanctity. So the church asks, "Want to meet God and be more holy? Have some bread, take some wine. Holy!"

Tomorrow, maybe you will eat breakfast differently.

In baptism, we make wild promises to God like, "I will raise this child to be a Christian," or "I will start thinking and acting as if I were a disciple."

But because baptism is something done to us rather than by us, our promises to God are responsive to the baptismal promises God makes to us in water: "I'll be your God. You'll be at home with me.

Get used to being drowned and born again and again until you more closely resemble the one I mean you to be."

When Jesus famously said, "Do this in remembrance of me," he meant "remember" not only as historical memory but also as, "Every time you eat together, wake up, remember who you are, open your eyes and see the holy amid the ordinary, sense my real presence with you at the table." In the sharing of bread and wine, we see the body of Christ, not only on the table in bread and wine, but at the table in God's gathering of God's family. Gift, all the way down.

SALVATION

The result of Christ's turn to us.

In horrible agony, the thief on the cross cried out to Jesus, "Save yourself and us." That's what Jesus did.

When Jesus invites himself to the home of Zacchaeus (worst man in town), and Zacchaeus responds with the most extravagant giveaway Jericho had ever seen, Jesus says, "Today salvation has come to this house." Not someday, somewhere. Here. Now. Salvation is whenever Jesus shows up and we start acting like it, giving it all we've got.

Although salvation is what God does without our contribution, salvation invites cooperation. A gift isn't much of a gift if it's refused. One of John's Wesley's favorite texts, "Work out your own salvation with fear in trembling," sent Calvinists and Lutherans through the roof. Still, though our salvation is a gift, Christ welcomes our response, our humble "yes" to his costly "Yes!"

Jesus advocated no program of human reform, recommended no collective social adjustments, no matter how badly needed or enlightened. Jesus was not into ethical codes, had no ideology, did no interesting work in political science and social ethics, and never put forth a plan of action, other than the seemingly wildly impractical notions that the first will be last, that we must turn the other cheek to those who strike us, forgive our enemies, find our lives by losing them, turn and become like little children.

What Jesus did was save us by adopting us into his family, the church, knowing that salvation is a group thing. Not waiting for people wanting to be saved, he sought them out for salvage. What did Jesus do as he lay three days in the tomb? First Peter says that he went to hell and preached to all who had never heard of him. Jesus is nothing if not salvific: from conception through ascension, for us and our salvation.

Jesus told a parable about workers who showed up early in the day to labor in the vineyard, while others didn't show up until midmorning, midday, even one hour before quitting time. At the end of the day, the quixotic boss paid everyone the same. There was grumbling. The landowner feigned surprise: "Why are you envious because of my generosity?"

I'll tell you why. We who have been lifelong Christians— attempting to follow Jesus from our youth, (against our desires) remaining chaste in our personal life, bored to tears by decades of Sunday school and long sermons—why should we not be envious when some little wayward lamb staggers back to the sheepfold, or a prodigal returns home? Salvation, when offered to the likes of you, provokes envy in me. Proffered to all comers, especially you latecomers, without regard for my merit, somehow salvation seems less gracious than God's grace reserved just for well-deserving me.

When Peter says that there is "no other name by which we must be saved," that's good news for anybody who needs saving; not so good for us, the entitled who are affronted by the scope of salvation in Jesus's name. Maybe that's why the church has traditionally taught that there is "no salvation outside the church." Salvation is a group thing, God taking us as a crowd, many of whom are not my type.

A major reason why a nice person like Jesus ended up on a cross was that he saved the wrong people, people who nobody thought could be saved, those that nobody even wanted saved.

SANCTIFICATION

Being turned more closely toward the God who has turned to us and thereby better resembling whom God means us to be.

The Gospels depict the disciples on a continual road trip. They journey, not only step-by-step closer to Jerusalem, but also day-by-day closer to Christ, that is, sanctification. Jesus takes us just as we are but doesn't leave us that way. If you sign on with Jesus, prepare to relocate.

Christ not only forgives; he renovates. Justification is the costly work that Christ does for you; sanctification is the continuing work that God does in you. We not only are saved by grace but are also enabled to grow in grace. A living God keeps remaking us even when we thought we were done. I'm not the most truthful, altruistic, antiracist person but, trust me, you wouldn't have wanted to know me before God got a grip.

Even Jesus "grew in wisdom and stature." Every time you surprise yourself by turning a bit closer to the God who has turned to you, it's a hint of your future self. Sanctification is to be drawn ever nearer to the God who has drawn near to us. God graciously promises: you don't have to resign yourself to the life your parents bred you to live; you can, by God's sanctifying grace working in you, expect more.

God loves us enough to take us as we are but promises to transform us into better people than we would have been if God had not had God's way with us. We excuse ourselves as poor, struggling sinners doing the best we can; Christ looks at us and sees saints, those who ought to be given an even greater role in advocating his coming reign.

Friendship with God, like human friendship, takes time. It's possible to be related to God in a moment; for most of us greater godliness is a long process. Our sin is so deeply rooted in our thinking and willing that only a lifetime of born-againings will do. Prayer, Bible reading, meditation, worship, singing, and serving are habits whereby we are drawn closer to God as God uses these means to draw near to us.

As John Wesley discovered, it's too much to expect ordinary people to be good, left to their own devises, but you can, by the grace of God, at least teach them good habits.

After the first Sabbath, God doesn't rest. If you are happy with yourself as a pig in mud, driven by a purposeful life, comprehend all of God that you care to know, and think you are living your best life now, keep looking over your shoulder. Be warned: God thinks you could be a saint.

And if you'd rather have happiness than holiness, if you don't really want to be a saint, be warned: the God of Israel and the church is accustomed to working with the disobliging.

SAVIOR

Who Jesus is and what he does.

When Jesus was born, an angel announced that this baby is the "Savior, who is Christ the Lord." Wrapped in rags, he sure didn't look like Lord of all, personification of God's great rescue operation. God becoming human "for us and our salvation," as the creed puts it, is God being most godly, God in action. Applying *savior* to Jesus is claiming that what Jesus does is God doing that which only God can do, evoking our indignant, "Who is this who forgives sins?"

The lonely love Jesus as a good friend. Jesus as the highest and best of humanity, a moral exemplar, is adored by we who think ourselves competent, responsible, and resourceful. Jesus the liberationist social activist is the favorite of those who long for a handle on power. Jesus the savior is best understood by the done-in, disoriented, drowning, dying, and desperate.

The gospel is more than religious experience, moral platitudes, strategy for straightening out the world, course of self-improvement, or appreciation for the wonders of nature, and better than a means of being comfortable in your own skin. The gospel is about a God who is for us and our salvation, the mighty act of God in history for the liberation of the cosmos so that the world might be returned to God. *Savior* is a name for God busy getting what God wants, redeeming the whole cosmos, including you as well as those you would as soon see lost as found.

SENTIMENTALITY

Substitution of a vague spiritual feeling for a crucified savior. Trivialization of evil. The delusion that if I sigh deeply and shed an empathetic tear of lament, I've actually done something. Cross-free discipleship. Sappy God substitute (in my particular church family).

Sentimentality denies our human enslavement to evil and sin, reducing the gospel to fantasies of earnest human striving, good intentions, and vague, positive feelings about ourselves and others. Sentimentality is the pretense of love without justice, forgiveness without reparations, affirmation by the Lord without judgment from the Lord. Rather than talk about a God who dares to justify the ungodly, we, the willfully innocent, boast of progressing toward godliness on our own. "We are fine just as we are, thank you, without need of divine intervention or costly makeover."

A mass killing? Do a candlelight vigil, link arms, and lie that "this community comes together in times like these."

Racism? "Find one person of another race and just have a café latte together. Discover the richness of this person's experience. You'll be blessed."

The essence of Christianity? "'Love your neighbor as yourself.'"

Death? "She will live on in our memories."

Sin? "I try to be a good person and help other people when I can and, after all, isn't that what religion is all about?"

Poverty? "Donate a used, but in good condition, bike for Christmas."

Closing line for a sermon? "Go forth. Work for justice, practice radical hospitality, love the lonely, welcome the stranger, and be kind to those in need. Amen."

If such sentimental drivel were true, how come Jesus was crucified?

When language is used for sentimental effect, particularly in church, the church forfeits its most valuable asset—truthful speech—for a cheap emotional rush and BS. Jesus on the cheap.

No cure for sentimentality other than unsentimental scripture. A pastor's job is not to put emotionally starved, lonely people in touch with their deeper feelings; we confront them with reality—the Trinity.

SEX

God invented it, saying, "I've enjoyed creating human life. Now, you try it. Be fruitful!"

Though a propagating activity of all living creatures, sex can be dangerous when done by humans. As with many of God's gifts, we pervert sex by entangling it with our self-deceit and our will to power or by elevating it to the level of a substitute sacrament.

Though sexual self-expression greatly concerns us consumer-driven Americans, and while churches split over issues of sexual orientation (bestowing upon sex an ontological significance God never gave it) sex is of seemingly little interest to Jesus. Dogs do it without instruction. Christ's nonchalance about sexual practice is another reminder that Jesus displayed a unique definition of what human beings are for.

Asked to comment on remarriage after divorce, Jesus implied that the important thing is fidelity, not sexual orientation. Promise-keeping is more demanding than coitus. Don't have sex with another person without first promising to be with that person no matter what.

Even though Paul is usually unhelpful when it comes to sexual ethics, Paul did say, "Glorify God in your body." Once Jesus made bread a moral, spiritual issue, why not genitals too? If God cares about our behavior in a board room, a sick room, or a classroom, it's understandable that God has opinions about what happens in a cheap motel room on the edge of town.

SIN

Turning everything into our personal benefit. Organizing the world around ourselves. Using rather than adoring God. The rules are made for everybody else. Me, center of the universe.

Looking for big-time sinners? Skip Vegas; look in church. Satan masquerades as an angel of light; church provides us sinners a clever cover. More importantly, Christians have a peculiar notion of sin and a weird idea of what God does with it.

We thought we were fairly nice people. Then Jesus commanded us to forgive repeatedly and to love our enemies. Suddenly, all looked like reprobates. Christian sin is not just a matter of deviating from a code of conduct, misuse of your power against another, a moral slipup, doing that which you know you should not. Sin is conscious and unconscious, seemingly innate human inclination to refuse to get on board with what God is up to in the world. Our failure to allow ourselves to be loved. Our inability to see Christ in the least of these. The sins of non-Christians are measly peccadillos by comparison.

Though Jesus named as sin that which everyone else regarded as normal male behavior (such as looking at a woman lustfully), nobody criticized Jesus for being too tough on sin; he was hounded for being too extravagant with forgiveness. Censured for the reprobates he hung out with, Christ defined his whole mission as calling sinners—only sinners—to repentance and fellowship. The sinners who bugged him most were good people who presumed themselves to be without sin.

Displaying little interest in the production of guilt or shame, Jesus enjoyed ruffling the feathers of the righteous with stories like that of the tax collector and the Pharisee at prayer. The self-righteous, Bible-believing Pharisee sat noticeably on the front pew and prayed, "God I thank you that I'm not like those sinners, especially that one on the back pew." The anything-but-righteous tax collector could only blurt out, "God show mercy to me, a sinner!" Guess who went home "justified"?

Christ promises not only to forgive but also to rebirth, offering the fresh start we can't give ourselves, and freedom to live lives no longer jerked around by sin. Who would condemn my random lustful thought? Or my brief burst of anger at the jerk who cut me off in traffic? Jesus, that's who, saying that to think it is as bad as doing it, promising that, given some time and the relentless work of the Holy Spirit, even I can more clearly resemble that one whom God has created me to be, making Paul exclaim, "Not I but Christ in me!"

Not content just to forgive us, Jesus commands us to be forgivers. God forgives you, God's enemy number one. Now, you try it. "Lord," says Peter, "how often shall I forgive my brother when he sins against me? As generously as seven times?" Jesus replies, "Not seven times but seventy times seven." That's a heap of repetitious forgiveness. Doesn't leave much time for condemning. A person could do nothing all day but forgive.

Atonement and *forgiveness* precede *sin*, in this book and in the Christian life. We're usually self-deceitful about our sin until we meet the one who says, "I've come to call sinners, only sinners." God's turning toward us makes us more cognizant of the ways that we have turned against God. Honesty about our sin is the fruit of relationship with a God who manages to be both gracious and truthful at the same time. Paul said that the good that he would do, he can't; the bad that he wouldn't do, he does. Paul wrote that *after* he met Christ.

As with death, only God can decisively defeat sin. Therefore, the cross. "Do your sinful worst," says Christ, "I can take it." Then, "Father, forgive, they don't know, have never known, will never know what they're doing." Looking through the lens of the cross of Christ, we see ourselves truthfully and call things by their proper names. The seriousness of our sin and what God does about it become manifest. Then, in the light of the resurrection, we see that God is determined not to let our sin defeat the purposes of God to save sinners, only sinners.

One of the gifts of the Christian faith is to be able to shed the defensive mask and to say with glad abandon, "Hello, I'm Will and I'm a sinner." Pity those anxious, overworked souls who think they've got to get it right, live a good life and be on the right side of every justice issue because nobody has told them the news, "Jesus Christ came to save sinners," only sinners.

If you are consumed by guilt, sinking so deep in sin that you think nothing can be done about it, it's important to remember that

Christianity is not about your sin. It's about Jesus. Don't take your sin more seriously than you take the promise, "Christ Jesus came into the world to save sinners."

SOLITUDE

The illusion that you are on your own and therefore in control of your thoughts just because you are sitting by yourself.

The Christian faith is inherently public, extroverted, and social because of Jesus. The Trinity shows us that God is better than omnipotent and omniscient; to the core, God is relational. Jesus relished the give-and-take of open debate and never backed down from a public argument. His ministry begins by gathering a group. When asked what God expected of us, Jesus offered a twofold command straight out of the decidedly communitarian faith of Israel—love God and your neighbor, implying that you can't love one without the other. If we are going to meet Jesus, grow in our relationship with him, and courageously obey him, it will be as members of his troupe, or not at all. That is, in church.

Christian worship is primarily communitarian—a group of companions around Jesus's table sharing good bread, good wine, and good conversation, not a poor soul eating silently, alone at Burger King. Safe, solitary, contemplative spirituality has its enthusiasts, but little biblical support.

True, there were a few times when Jesus went alone to the desert to pray, but we don't know what happened in his solitude except in Gethsemane. There, Jesus was forced into isolation by the evil that lay before him. In solitude he was beset by his greatest temptation.

More typical is for Jesus to be constantly mixing it up with a crowd, accosting travelers on the road, fostering uncomfortable conversations, and most scandalously of all, eating, drinking, and carousing indiscriminately with both friends and enemies. In more than one of his parables, Jesus depicted God's kingdom as a shindig. When just one little wayward lamb finally is found, heaven goes wild: "Let's party!"

Jesus's rich social life implies that if we are to be fully human, it will not be in separateness but through a public web of relationships, responsibilities, and connections with others, including God. Puff out your chest saying, "I gotta be me," strip yourself of your commitments to others, and what's left will be less than the you God has in mind. This faith is ill-sung solo.

Yes, God in Jesus Christ can be encountered in solitary walks in the woods or by sitting alone and reading a book (!). More typical is for convivial Christ to show up at a dinnertime doing what he loved—sharing food, drink, and truth in conversation with friends. Christ says, "Where two or three are gathered, count me in."

SON OF MAN OR HUMAN ONE

A name for the humanity of Christ, counterpart to Son of God. Can also refer to a strange, eschatological figure whose appearance indicates the end of history, the beginning of last judgment, God setting things right.

Mark speaks of the Son of Man coming in clouds with great glory. Jesus as a fully present, humble human being and at the same time the feared, hoped-for judgment and righteousness of God is a mystery Christians would rather anticipate than explain.

SPIRITUALITY

There's more going on than you know.

While you read these words, God is doing more in you than you can say. Brave souls explore the more, venturing beyond the limits of taste, sense, sight, and consciousness, trailing Jesus into the un-known, in spite of their misgivings: that's spirituality.

The flat, humdrum ho hum that passes for worship in many congregations, along with inconsequential preaching, account for the rash of goofy spiritualities of this and that. When spirituality floats free from the spirit of Christ, it blurs and becomes an excuse for a nose-dive into subjectivity. Spirituality becomes how I'm feeling when I'm feeling particularly good about me. Who needs more of that?

The challenge in being spiritual is to keep tethered to the Holy Spirit, the spirit of Christ, rather than to burrow into the recesses of the unfocused, insolent, self-concerned human spirit.

Scripture can help test the spirits. In scripture, the Holy Spirit rests on bodies—the body of Christ in his baptism, the body of be-lievers at Pentecost. In a faith that's more solidly material and incar-national than fluffily ethereal, the church and its scripture help keep spirituality from degenerating into the private and the amorphous. If it's not the spirit of love, it's not the Holy Spirit.

Those who say that they are "spiritual but not religious," who claim to feel more spiritual at home watching others do church on a screen rather than bothering with the messiness of Christ's body, are right. Spirit is easier to get along with than the Holy Spirit.

Practitioners of spirituality ought always to remember that it was to the spiritually deficient that Jesus gave his blessing and his kingdom, forever annoying those of us who get paid to be spiritual.

THEOLOGY

Talk by, about, and to God.

Dare ask, "Why me?" or "What did I do to deserve this?" or "That's not God, is it?" and you are calling for theology. Occasionally done by a few professors for pay, theology is the normal, unavoidable pursuit of average Christians too. The unexpectedness of Jesus, human life in all its wonder and sadness, makes theologians of us all. Theology's sphere of interest? Everything. As creator of all, the God of Israel and the church has opinions about the whole shebang.

At some point in the modern age, theology ceased being adventurous human attempts to hear talk by God and became introverted human commentary on human experience of God. Anthropology (talk about ourselves) is easier than theology, which explains why so many sermons are too focused on us and too little concerned with God.

Sometimes theology is literary malpractice, a tortured intellectual defense against Jesus rather than a means of coming closer to him. "Let's all sit around and have an interesting discussion of concepts about Jesus rather than get off our duffs and follow him." "Systematic theology" falsifies its subject; Jesus is a complex person rather than an orderly dogmatic system. "Contextual theology" betrays the inability of its practitioners to climb out of their social, political, gender, ethnic context long enough to talk about God rather than themselves. "Constructive theology" has usually been known as idolatry.

All theology is "practical theology," belief put into practice, or it isn't worth the bother. A theologian came up to Jesus proposing a debate on "eternal life." At first Jesus brushes him off with an answer everybody already knew: love God with everything you've got and your neighbor as much as you love yourself.

"So, rabbi, just who is my neighbor?" the man persisted.

Not, "Who is this God I'm to love with all my heart, soul, mind, and strength?" He asked, "Who is my neighbor?" hoping to draw Jesus into a dispute about ascertaining deserving from undeserving neighbors.

Refusing to be tricked into a theological bull session, Jesus responded with his parable of the good Samaritan, ending with, "Go . . . do."

At its best, theology serves the church by testing our talk about God to make sure that the God we are talking about is the same who meets us as Christ rather than more pliable godlets of our concoction. This may explain why many of us are nervous around theologians.

TRINITY

God the Father almighty is God. Jesus the Jew from Nazareth is God. The Holy Spirit that descended upon the church at Pentecost is God. There's only one God.

A favorite ploy for keeping God off our backs is to render God distant, vague, and static—and therefore irrelevant. God made simple, abstract, impersonal, and inactive is a God who will never catch you off guard or make you ill-at-ease. When most Americans say "God," they are referring to a dim, cold generalization other than the threefold God who turned toward us in Jesus Christ.

Once we discovered that God was in Christ, things got complicated, not because the church wanted to make sweet, simple Jesus complex and confusing but because we discovered in Jesus that God is more demanding and much more interesting than we first thought. We had to expand our notions of God. Jesus was "conceived by the Holy Spirit," born of a peasant woman in Judea, teaching, working wonders among us in the "power of the spirit," constantly conversing with his Father about us, suffering and dying at our hand, rising after three days and returning to us, and breathing the Holy Spirit upon us—well, we realized that we didn't know what we were talking about when we had said "God." Only a trinitarian God—both distinctly three and yet harmonious and united—adequately describes what happens in the incarnation. There's no way we could have made it up on our own. These three are one.

God as an impersonal power, a monad, a fair-minded, balanced cosmic bureaucrat who dispassionately administers natural law from the safe distance of eternity, is easier to get along with than the intensely communal, unreservedly personal, too-close-for comfort Trinity.

Trinitarian thinking keeps God as complicated but also as unified as God is. Most heresies are the result of misguided attempts to smooth over that which we find too difficult in the Trinity, to relax the tensions produced by the paradox of an utterly one God who is at the same time distinctively Father, uniquely Son, and vividly Holy Spirit.

A particularly delightful—and sometimes exasperating—aspect of the Trinity is God's loquaciousness. Father, Son, and Holy Spirit are in complete communion and constant communication, the Father directly speaking to the Son, the Son communicating with the Father, all in the power of the Holy Spirit. There is a divine overflowing, revelatory generosity, and effervescence in the way the Trinity relates to us creatures, the Father creatively addressing creation, the Son talking to the Father and the Holy Spirit about us, the Holy Spirit delivering the self-communication of the Father and Son back to us. The Trinity's oneness is relational, which implies that, as those created in the "image of God," we're meant to be relational too.

TROUBLEMAKER

Not a biblical term for Jesus or his followers, but it should be.

Who would take the trouble to crucify somebody who said only, "Consider the lilies"? Something about who Jesus was, what he was

131

up to and what he said made most people turn away. His own family thought he was nuts. A chief charge against the first evangelists was, "They are turning the world upside down."

Showing no respect for authorities, governmental or religious, Jesus called them "blind fools," "full of extortion," "evil and adulterous," "brood of vipers," "viscious wolves." When criticized for the company he kept, Jesus's response was uncivil: "I didn't come to call righteous people, but sinners." What's your mission, Jesus? "To cast fire upon the earth." "Don't think that I've come to bring peace."

When you think about it, the wonder is not that the bigwigs killed Jesus but that it took them three years to do it. Maybe we privileged and powerful are always slow to get the point.

If you simply must have your preaching balanced, orderly, civil, and careful not to rock your boat, find a preacher with greater reverence for the status quo than Jesus. You won't have to look far. People-pleasing preachers with theological training that enables them to be less obnoxious than Jesus are a dime a dozen. It's troubling that too few churches are in trouble.

TRUTH

Not only what Jesus teaches but also who Jesus is.

You're reading this book because as a follower of Jesus you must tell the truth, so far as truth has been given to you by the one who was not only the way, the life, but also truth. True, there's little evidence for believing that the world wants truth any more than it wanted Jesus. It's bad enough that our politicians lie; worse, we eat it up and excuse their untruthfulness.

When Jesus says that he is a witness to the truth, urbane, classically educated Pilate asks, "What is truth?," perhaps hoping to escape culpability for the violent injustice that he was too cowardly to stop.

A favorite ruse for getting rid of this stripped, whipped Son of God is to go philosophical and abstract: I've got my truth; you've got yours. It's not a lie if you sincerely think it's true. Gospel news is fake. It's arrogant for you to believe that you've been given truth that is truthier than mine. Your "truth" is but a commentary on your will-to-power-cramming of your truth down everybody else's throat. Truth is relative to your cultural (or gender, racial, national, generational, economic, etc.) context, not to what's actually true. What is truth?

Jesus didn't give answer to Pilate's truth question; Christ is the answer. Christian truth is a Jew from Nazareth. Jesus has come not to tell us some truth nor to list a set of absolute, free-standing truths. "I am the truth," he says. The whole truth and nothing but the truth about God and each of us has a face, a name: Jesus Christ, truth personified, embodied, moving in on us, revealing, speaking, truth in action, truth that chooses rather than is chosen, truth refusing to be abstract, unknowable, or impractical.

As Christ's body, the church is called primarily not for friendliness, community, fellowship, or social justice. The church is sacred, free space where, in a culture of lies, we gather in the name of the truth to tell the truth. Pastors are called to be more than hand-holding toadies; we are preachers who open the scriptures and speak the truth that people can't get elsewhere.

Here's some good news. If you've been conned into excusing and defending the lies of some immoral president, don't lie about your lapse in good judgment. Jesus loves to forgive.

Truth makes us free. Paul tells the church that the only way to grow up "into Christ" is to speak "the truth in love." Whether spoken in spite or in love, the truth can still make you uncomfortable. Maybe that's why too many congregations reward their preachers for equivocation and punish them for pulpit veracity, opting to be a warm-hearted fellowship of niceness rather than people of the truth.

UNITY

Together, in Christ.

If Christ were content to atone, that is reconcile and unite us
to God, the worship of Christ would be all praise and adoration.
Instead, he set before us a table of his body and blood, a communal
meal as sign of his intentions and invited all comers to his banquet
without consulting us about the guest list. Jesus makes us begin his
prayer by saying, "Our Father" rather than "My Father." If we are to
be saved, it will be as a group. Jesus's longest prayer was that all of his
followers might be one.

Still, one of the most difficult things to love about Jesus is his
determination to save people whom we don't like. "Love each other
as I have loved you," has, from the first, been one of Jesus's most
difficult commands. He probably meant love among his disciples
rather than love of humanity in general, which may seem a limitation
of the love's scope unless you have tried to make love in church. If
there's one thing tougher than loving your neighbor of another faith
who lives half way around the world, it's loving your fellow church
member with whom you are stuck on the parish finance committee.

I estimate that at least a third of Paul's letters deal with issues
of church splits and fights. Paul wouldn't have written his great
hymn to love if First Church Corinth had been united. After some
ingratiating sweet talk and high-flown theology, Paul blurts out
what's really bugging him about the Philippians, "Be reconciled!"

Paul tells the Corinthians that he hears that their congregation
is divided, which may not be all bad. Disunity can be an honest admission of our differences, testimony to Christ's propensity to convene people even when we don't get along with each other. Limit
the church to folk of one race, or the same economic group, you'll
have unity but not that of Christ. If there's one thing worse than a

fragmented congregation, it's one where people are forced to shut up and suppress their disagreements in order to put up a united front.

Unity should not be purchased by lying: To those of us who have said, "I've never seen America more disunited. We've got to come together," the Black church responds, "American unity? We must have missed that."

At the foot of the cross, we look much the same and even from the cross, Jesus continued to make community. Though disputes and division characterized Jesus's first disciples, Jesus constantly commanded them to work for unity and community, never once glorifying or providing theological justification for separation and schism. Maybe that's why anybody who splits a church, walks out of a congregation, or forms a breakaway denomination always cites the best of reasons: biblical authority, purity of doctrine, compassion for all, marriage and family, holier than thou, blah, blah, blah. By their arguments they show they are nervous about their disunion, knowing down deep that Jesus will have none of it.

UNIVERSALISM

The hope that all will be saved.

If God has found a way to turn toward you, enabling you to turn toward God, it's charitable of you to believe that God is able to turn to any and all and that they shall all turn to God. Once Jesus showed up and calls a wretch like you, it's hard not to be a universalist.

Still, some ask, "Will *all* be saved?" In one sense, such speculation is none of our business. Only God does salvation.

On the other hand, it's important to believe that the benevolence Christ has shown you is shown toward all, without limiting the extravagance of God. You don't get to disapprove of the way God loves humanity. Your job is to make sure that everyone gets the news of the Trinity's universal intent.

Christ has been given all. God was in Christ, reconciling the whole world to himself. Paul says that just as all have sinned, so has God shown mercy to all. All. As in Adam, all die, so in Christ shall all be made alive. All.

First Timothy says that God desires that all be saved. Whether or not all will be saved (God's self-assigned task) and turn toward God (we can't know just who has and has not adequately responded to God), we ought at least to hope that all be saved, since we ought to want what God wants. What does God want? All.

Though Jesus Christ is Lord, God doesn't always get what God wants. Human sin presupposes itself. God has made us free for God's love yet also free stupidly to resist. Who knows the full extent of human idiocy? Could human refusal overpower God's relentless resurrection resourcefulness?

In the parable of the waiting father, the father yearns to welcome but doesn't force the prodigal to return home nor coerce the older brother to loosen up and join the father's party. God enables, encourages, empowers human response to God, but if God coerced us to return God's love, would it be love?

Let's be honest. Sometimes others don't embrace God's love in Christ, not because they rejected Christ, but because they are put off by the rotten way the church has presented God.

Though we don't know the limits of humanity's power to reject the God who has refused to reject humanity, having seen—in Christ's resurrection—God refuse our rejection, disallowing our decisions as the final word on relations between God and us, we wonder, just how decisive can human rejection be?

Jesus told a parable about a last, universal judgement when "all the nations will be gathered in front of him." The goats aren't separated from the sheep on the basis of their belief or profession of faith but because of their visits to prison, and work at the food bank and clothes closet. Good news! In as much as you did the good that you could for his little ones, you were doing it to Jesus.

Both the sheep and the goats are clueless. "Lord, we can't recall ever having seen you." To us has not been given the insight into just who is a sheep and who is a goat, nor do we know the ultimate significance of the good that we do nor the ways Jesus works incognito. But Jesus always knows us.

Just when we smugly settle down safe in the sheepfold, the good shepherd says, "I've got sheep who are not yet in the fold. You don't know them, but I do. And, if it's the last thing I do, I'll bring them in too!" That's Jesus for you.

"Will all be saved?" We have reason to hope that God will at last achieve that which God desires, that for which God has so dearly paid. We can pray that God's will be done for all, as it has been done in us. We can work for universal fulfillment of God's desire. All we know for sure is that God was in Christ, reconciling the whole— sometimes responding, often rebelling—world to himself.

Besides, who wants to show up in eternity, stand before the throne of God, and be embarrassed by having the almighty ask, "Nice to see you, but where are the others?"

VIOLENCE

The world's way of accomplishing good.

When a squad of soldiers come to arrest an unarmed rabbi, Peter—the rock upon which Jesus promised to build his church— whips out his sword and nicks a bit off an ear, showing that he is as inept at swordplay as discipleship. Earlier Jesus had commanded his disciples to go forth unarmed. But in the dark, when the going gets rough, you can't tell the difference between Caesar's lackeys and the disciples of Jesus—we've all got swords.

Jesus cursed Peter: "Put the sword back. . . . All those who use the sword will die by the sword." That evening, Jesus prohibited his disciples from practicing self-defense, never rescinding his prohibition.

Those who take the sword will die by it; this is one of Jesus's truest proverbs. Both victor and vanquished fanaticize that the sword is our only means of security. As all nations know, there's no way to get anything important done without swords. Why does the United States have the most expensive military in the world? Peace. Why so many guns on our streets? Love for our families.

If Jesus had only said the innocuous, "Treat people in the same way that you want them to treat you," everybody would follow him. Unfortunately for those of us in a world at war, Jesus said, "If someone slaps you on your right cheek, you must turn the left cheek to them as well." A Roman soldier commands, "Jew, carry my pack a mile," take it a mile more. Pray for your enemies! Bless those who harass you! Don't resist the evil one!"

If Jesus had backed up these orders with something silly like, "Turning the other cheek will bring out the best in your enemies and make your attacker less violent," then one could accuse Jesus of being goofily idealistic or sappily sentimental.

Jesus's justification was twofold: (1) do this because I do it, and (2) deal with others as God deals with you. Can we arm ourselves to the teeth to hurt those who threaten to hurt us when God is nonviolently kind to the ungrateful and the selfish and causes sun to shine on the good and the bad? Violence was the way the world reacted to Jesus, never, not once, the way Jesus reacted to the world. Jesus, the only "prince," not in uniform.

"Freedom is not free," says a military recruitment poster. The church replies, the sacrifice of Christ ended sacrifice of our children to war in order to secure our freedom.

Jesus's prohibition of arms has always elicited fancy intellectual footwork from those who desire somehow to enlist Jesus into our crusades and military adventures. Defenders of "just war" and "Christian realism" have found Jesus to be not only nonviolent but also uncooperative.

VOCATION

Called, assigned, enlisted, commissioned by God.

Jesus begins his ministry by calling twelve none-too-talented yokels, declaring that what he wants to accomplish in the world he'll do through them. Jesus ends his ministry not with reassurance but with assignment: Go! Get out of here and make me disciples, baptizing, and teaching them all that I have commanded. The savior is delegator.

Saul was quite happy with his life, on his way to defend God's honor from wacko followers of the Way. On the way, Saul is knocked down by the risen Christ.

"Saul, Saul, why are you persecuting me?" (When God calls, it often takes a couple of times before those being called figure out that it's God.)

When Christ explains to Ananias his appearance to religious terrorist Saul, Christ mentions neither forgiveness of Saul's sins nor peace, purpose, and prosperity, only that he gave Saul a job—taking Christ's name even to Gentiles and kings. "I will show him how much he must suffer for the sake of my name." Saul thought he knew suffering but when he became Paul and started working for Jesus, Paul found that Jesus routinely makes life more difficult for people by deploying them in his mission.

"Who will go for us?" young Isaiah hears heaven ask during a service at the temple.

"I'm here. Send me!" he responds, without the foggiest idea of what he's getting into. But then Isaiah remembers all of the good reasons why he would make a lousy prophet: "I'm ruined! I'm a man of unclean lips and I live among a people of unclean lips."

Immediately a heavenly being takes a hot coal from the altar and scorches Isaiah's lips. See? God equips those whom God calls, though it may be unpleasant for the one who is called.

The life you are living is not your own. You are salvaged from the conventional American, "What do I want to do with me?" and thrust into asking the more countercultural, "Which God am I worshipping, and how is that God is having God's way with me?"

We belong to God, to be utilized as God pleases. All the baptized are obligated to serve Christ in whatever we do: in the New Testament, "calling" or "vocation" refers to deployment rather than employment. We can be called to "eternal life," or into fellowship with Christ, out of darkness into light, and into right relationship with God, but not necessarily to a career. You can retire from your job, but not from discipleship.

Vocation is good news that you have been given a bit part to play in God's world reclamation. If you've been blessed, now you are given the means to do something meaningful with your stuff. If you've got pain, you're given responsibility for someone else's pain, thus allowing you the freedom not to obsess on your own wounds. You are delivered from the burden of having to make up the significance of your life on your own. You don't have to work hard to choose yourself into the good life; in calling, assigning, utilizing you, Christ makes your life count.

Choosing you doesn't mean that God has chosen you for blessing and others are rejected. It just means that you have been chosen for a role, a task whereby God blesses others through you. As Jesus told his disciples, "You didn't choose me, I chose you." Why? "So that you could go and produce fruit."

And if the time is not right for you to be called, or if you have grave reservations about your ability to do God's work, don't want God to mess with your lips, or are beset by personal doubts or insecurities, or if you are not in the best of health, or burdened by financial cares, God doesn't care.

WAIT

"I hope, LORD.
My whole being hopes,
and I wait for God's promise."

God is not on demand. Much of the Christian life is spent waiting. God turns toward us, but usually not immediately. Those who wait upon the Lord shall renew their strength and rise up like eagles. But for now, we chickens roost on some random perch and wait.

Sometimes in church the pastor says, "God is good, all the time," and the congregation piously responds, "All the time, God is good." Trouble is, God is good, but not always on our schedule. A sovereign God is free to come and go. Grace is not a gift if it's predictably at our beck and call. We wait in hope for the cancer to be healed, for the virgin birth of Jesus to make sense, to be given the grace to forgive, for the kids to turn out okay, for God to be God in God's fullness. God's promises have been made, but all promises are in the future tense and rarely are they completely fulfilled as soon as we'd like.

Waiting can be one of the toughest jobs of disciples, particularly for those of us who are at the age when we have more yesterdays than tomorrows on our account. Patience may be a requisite Christian virtue, though a virtue that God has not seen fit to give me. I wait for the ability patiently to wait.

"Lazarus whom you love is dying. Lord, come quickly," beg Mary and Martha. Jesus remains where he is for three days. When

Jesus finally gets done with whatever he is doing and arrives at the cemetery, it's all over.

Why did Jesus delay three days before coming to the aid of his friends? To allow Lazarus to die so that Jesus could resuscitate him and impress people with his life-giving power? To teach Mary and Martha patience? As foreshadowing of Jesus's three days in the tomb?

Who knows? After all, it's the Gospel of John. We know that the agonizing wait had to be hard on Mary and Martha, as tough as for the watchman who wait for the morning.

What happens when we die? Most Christians seem to believe that the moment you die, you go immediately to be with Jesus. And there's biblical justification for thinking that. More typical of historic Christian thought is that when you die you wait on the trumpet's sound and God's resurrection of all the dead. As in life, so in death, we wait. Pagans called their burial place "necropolis," city of the dead. Christians called it "cemetery," place of anticipatory sleep. We wait because awakening to eternity is only God's to give. The next move is up to God.

Waiting is a sign that you know that what you need is not yet yours. The world, as good as it often is, is not as good as creation can get, and you are not yet the new creature God intends you to be. Though God has given us a good world and Jesus has wrought our salvation, there's more to come. It took God a whole six days to create the world. The Hebrews were enslaved for four hundred years before God's liberation. Today we wait.

Our waiting for God may seem like time wasted whereas to God it's taking enough time to do what God wants to accomplish. Besides, with God, a thousand years is as one day of our waiting. There, feel better now?

Jesus told a parable about an unproductive fig tree. Three years, no figs. "Cut it down!" says the landowner.

"Give it more time," pleads the servant. "Put manure on it. Maybe the dung will do it."

What seems to us only muck piled higher is God's gift of time. By taking time, God gives us space to mature, to develop, to grow in wisdom and stature, just like little Jesus. Friendship requires time. God waits, the father of the prodigal waiting for his son to come to his senses and turn back toward home. Maybe God waits to bring it all to conclusion because God is unsatisfied with just you and me; God wants as vast a multitude as possible to enjoy eternity.

Not quite ready to turn toward the God who has turned toward you? "No problem," says God, "I've got all the time in the world."

WALK

Before Jesus called his disciples to believe, love, or to trust him, Jesus invited them just to walk with him.

Paul remembers Abraham as "walking in the way of trust," out of the blue commanded by God to go to a land "that I will show you." Abraham walked away from his accustomed security and all that he relied upon—family, friends, flocks—walking toward an unknown place. "He went as the Lord told him." Then there's the long, wordless walk Abraham took with his only begotten son Isaac up Mount Moriah. Walking away from what he knew toward what he didn't has made Abraham a faith hero of everybody who has been made an immigrant by Christ's "Follow me." The Christian life is less a meditative, reflective time apart than a journey from here to there, leaving what you know, heading out to where God only knows.

Paul praised those who run with perseverance. But many of us have found the Christian life to be more a slow, step-by-step amble than a hundred-yard dash. Sometimes we speak of working for and serving with Jesus, believing in and speaking up for Jesus. It's nice to know that just walking—actively but unspectacularly putting one foot in front of the other, trusting that God is leading us to God knows where—is also "faith."

Take heart: the father of the prodigal didn't just walk toward the returning son who had walked out on him—he ran.

WEALTH

Having too much stuff for your own good.

While we would like to know more about Jesus, one thing we know for sure; Jesus knew that rich people are in big trouble. Never did Jesus praise wealth as a result of hard work, the art of the deal, or divine blessing. More typically he spoke of riches as either sorry fruit of foolishness or temptation to godlessness.

Of all the people Jesus calls, "Follow me!" only one refused. Let those of us blessed and cursed by riches note: the man's rebuff of discipleship was due to money. If we would enter the kingdom of God, Jesus insists that we travel light.

Since God is going to rip off our stuff anyway (otherwise known as death), it's probably a good idea to begin divesting now, foretaste of when none of us will have any power, honor, or wealth because it all belongs to the Lamb.

WITNESS

Telling and showing the news we've heard and seen about God.

A witness's value is not intelligence or disposition. All that's wanted of a witness is, "Tell the court what you saw and heard."

Witness is the main job to which Jesus assigns us. He calls us not to grant a privilege; he summons us in order to commission us as witnesses, drawing us to him in order to send us out to tell all the world about him.

When the women came to the tomb on Easter morning, the angel didn't say, "He is risen! Now you will see your loved ones after you die." The command was, "Go, tell!"

The chief purpose of clergy is to "equip the saints" for their work as witnesses. That's why this book defining the words of faith is worth whatever you paid for it. Trust me. I'm giving you the words you'll need to witness over a cup of coffee, or before a judge's bench, across a garden fence, or if you're handed a bullhorn in a Black Lives Matter demonstration.

Truth to tell, few people are turned off by Jesus because of Jesus; most turn away from him because of our pathetic witness. We got the words right, but not the moves. They dismiss us with, "You must look more redeemed if I am to believe in your redeemer."

Still, if the world is going to know the truth about God, it will be through us witnesses. In the Gospel of John Jesus says he is the light of the world. In Matthew, Jesus looks upon his ragtag followers, knows their faults and flaws, and still says, "You are the light of the world. Shine!"

Warning: "Martyr" comes directly from the Greek for "witness."

WORLD

God not only made it, but relentlessly, steadfastly sticks with it, and loves to make and remake it.

Jesus didn't die for the church; what he did, he did for all. Jesus is the way God loves the world, commanding us to be in the world in the same way because the world doesn't know it's God's without someone to show and tell.

At the same time, the church is to be in but not of the world, to love the world the way Christ loves it—confronting what's wrong with the world and refusing to sit by as the world is less than God intends it to be. Christ came into the world, God's great yes, and the world responded with a violent *no*. Followers of Christ are sent into the world to give the world the news that it's God's world. The world responds by making discipleship downright sheep-amid-wolves dangerous.

Sometimes, in attempting to obey Christ and reach out to the world, the church falls face down in the world so that you can't tell the difference between church and world. In the resulting parody, nothing is said that the world couldn't hear elsewhere. The line between church and Rotary is blurred. Rotary at least meets at a convenient hour and serves lunch.

When it's hard to tell a Christian from your average thinking, caring, sensitive American, when Christian positions are little better than the Republican (or Democratic) Party at prayer, who cares? In attempting to lure the world, the church got caught and caged by the world.

WORSHIP

Reflexive wonder, love, and praise. Responsive human words and deeds prompted by God's having turned toward us.

The big question is not how or when we'll worship but whom. Idolatry—praising, and adoring something other than the God who has turned to us—is easier. The hard part of worship is not sitting through a dull service and enduring second-rate music but rather the fearful possibility of falling into the hands of a living God, becoming like the one we adore, and hearing a word we would never say to ourselves.

The risk in Christian worship is the Trinity. The prophet Amos had the unpleasant task of telling Israel that Yahweh hated their high holy days and was bored to tears by the eleven o'clock service, the stewardship minute, praise song racket, and the morbid organ postlude. The worship God wants is a deluge of justice, a river of righteousness.

Button-down keepers of propriety get nervous when worship becomes Pentecostal. Ecstasy occurs (from the Greek *ekstasis*, to stand outside oneself—so difficult for self-absorbed people like us). Uptight people are given free space for unselfconscious frolic, the beaten down and the voiceless stand and shout as loudly as they please, the stoic are embarrassed when an involuntary tear trickles down their cheek, and the simple are lured into deep notions they would never have thought up on their own. We say with Jacob, when heaven's ladder was lowered within his reach, "The Lord was definitely in this place, and I didn't know it!"

It's deliciously nonutilitarian. We don't sing songs of praise or lament to the high heavens in order to get somewhere with God; we sing as those who have arrived. There's a gratuitous quality to Sunday morning liturgy—overstatement, repetition, extravagance, parading about in fancy dress, dancing, and full-throttle emotion—the way lovers sing songs or write poems for their beloved even when they are no good at poetry or can't carry a tune. The goofiness of lovers is difficult to explain to those who've never been in love.

Because it's not easy to greet or to be in conversation with a living God, Christians tend to engage in predictable ritual, doing and saying the same things repetitively, week-in, week-out. Habit helps us not to obsess about how well we are doing so that we are free to think about what God is doing. Ritual gives us the guts to come before the throne of God, without having to think about it, to stand at the foot of the cross of Christ, to set ourselves in that space where the living God may surprise us.

Sometimes the world accuses us of escapism—worship as narcotic, anesthetic respite from reality—misunderstanding how our rites can be risky acts of defiant imagination, whereby, just for a few moments on Sunday, the roof is blown off the building, and we are given a glimpse of a new heaven and new earth, new you, new me. We join our voices with people we don't know that well, only to be surprised that when we come with them to the Lord's Table, we're family. We never again look at them or bread in the same way.

"Yes!" we exclaim. "For this we were created. This is where we are headed. Yes! World as God expects it to be. Yes! Me as I'm becoming. Yes! It all makes sense. Yes! Where do I sign up for the cross? Jesus, count me in!"

For a glorious, gifted moment, we stand outside ourselves, lost in wonder, love, and praise that points toward home.

XENOPHOBIA

Fearing foreigners, no matter what Jesus says.

Jesus Christ cares nothing for boundaries, walls, and human division. He talks to anybody and saves everybody regardless of nationality, gender, race, or other ways we draw lines between ourselves in order to build ourselves up and to put others down. There may be good reasons for a border wall in Jerusalem or in Texas; Jesus Christ is not one of them.

Good Jew that he is, Jesus knew that God expects Israel to receive the stranger, commanding followers to welcome the outsider, declaring that when we receive the other, we receive him, charging us to step over every boundary, burst all barriers, and tell the truth about God's relentless determination to have everyone join the party called kingdom of God. To regard another as a threat or illegal alien is a commentary on how badly we've compromised our faith in Jesus and truncated his salvation.

Just when we're settling in with nice folks like us in our cozy church club, Jesus says that he's got others who belong to his flock whom we haven't met. We don't know them, but he does; he is discontent until they've immigrated into his kingdom. We can either hunker down with those with whom we are most comfortable in the flock or we can join Jesus's search for the others.

Xenophobia, fear of the other, is usually a sign that we have taken the USA or EU more seriously than we take membership in God's family. Sad behavior for those who, by baptism, are naturalized citizens of the kingdom of God, undocumented aliens brought over borders by Jesus.

YHWH

God's self-designation.

When God shows up to Moses, speaking as a burning bush that isn't consumed, it's been so long since anybody has worshipped the true and living God that we forgot God's name. "I Am Who I Am," replies God, or if you prefer, "I Will Be Who I Will Be." In the Hebrew text: YHWH. Tossing in vowels, Yahweh.

To call yourself "I Am" suggests that God's name is beyond naming. God will not be as we would have God to be but as God is. God will not be defined, named, and designated by us and thereby ordered around. God will be who God will be whether we like it or not. We can't call God whatever we please. As the angel orders Joseph, "You will call his name Jesus, the one who saves," rather than, "Josh, the therapist" or "Manny, the masseur."

Still, God loves us enough to give us God's name. In our times of privation, we need not incoherently mumble, "O great, incomprehensible, unknowable, impersonal Some One who may or may not be out there somewhere." We have been entrusted with the proper name whereby we, even we, can call upon the name of the Lord. We are given the privilege of being on a first name basis with the Son of God, able to pray in Jesus's name, even to begin prayer with "Our Father." Abba. Paul names as "saved" anyone who calls the Lord by name.

ZACCHAEUS

On his way to the cross, Jesus goes through Jericho. A man whose first name begins with the last letter of the ABCs climbs up a sycamore to get a look at the notorious rabbi.

Zacchaeus must climb up because "he was short." Whether "he" refers to the stature of Jesus or of Zacchaeus, who knows? (Short Jesus or short Zacchaeus, I've got a sermon on either.)

Then the shock: Jesus tells Zacchaeus to come down from the tree and brashly invites himself to Zacchaeus's house for lunch. The crowd is scandalized. Good, religious, but not showy mainliners like us, they grumble, "He's gone to be a guest at the house of a sinner!"

"Sinner" isn't the half of it. Zacchaeus isn't just a sinner; he is a tax collector, a quisling collaborating with the Romans to fleece kith and kin by raising money for the occupation forces, skimming off the top for himself. The chief of all the tax collectors. Short, he may be, but he's the biggest sinner in town.

And Zacchaeus is the only person Jesus visits in Jericho.

Once the food is served, Zacchaeus launches into a toast: "I'm so honored that you have chosen to dine at my house. To prove it, I give half of all I own to the poor. And if it can be shown that I've cheated anyone," (the little wretch has defrauded everybody in town at one time or another) "I'll repay four times as much, I'll . . . "

Jesus interrupts Zacchaeus's pious speech by blurting out, "Today salvation has come to this house because (let me repeat this one more time since you didn't get it four chapters ago) the Human One has come to seek and to save the lost."

To witness Jesus turning to the worst sinner in town, instantly turning him into the biggest do-gooder this town's ever seen, well, it's more than us moderately religious, trying-to-do-a-little-good-when-we-can Jerichoan Methodists can take: joy for the lost, grumbling among the found.

Dining as the guest of the worst sinner in town is one of the few times that Jesus speaks of "salvation." "Saved" is whenever and wherever Jesus invites himself to dine at your table. Not a future possibility but a present reality. Salvation here, now.

At the end of our ABCs it's good to be reminded that without awaiting our invitation, Jesus intrudes, bends toward us, assumes the task of seeking and saving the lost. You don't need to go looking for Jesus; he'll find you. You don't return to him; he'll turn to you and, when salvation comes to your house, as Jesus makes your table his, you'll then quite freely turn to him.

Zacchaeus urges me to add this: though Christ's salvation is free, it may cost you an arm and a leg.

Pathways to Follow

If you are a church leader or pastor, or if you are reading this book as an individual or with a group, here are some ABCs for Christians, organized thematically as suggested paths for your journey:

What is the significance of Jesus Christ?

Atonement, God, Incarnation, Lord, Lord's Prayer, Messiah, Parable, Paul, Reconciliation, Resurrection, Salvation, Savior, Son of Man/Human One, Trinity, Troublemaker

If you are an inquirer and want to know more about the Christian faith, you might read these entries:

Atheism, Certitude, Christian, Church, Conversion, Discipleship, Evangelism, Faith, God, Salvation, Vocation

If you are an experienced Christian who wants to grow in your faith, these words may stimulate your growth:

Apocalyptic, Atonement, Church, Conversion, Covenant, Discipleship, Election, Eschatology, Eternal Life, Evangelism,

153

Faith, Forgiveness, Holiness, Incarnation, Judgment, Justification, Kingdom of God, Mission, Pelagian, Providence, Realism, Reconciliation, Revelation, Sanctification, Theology, Trinity, Truth, Universalism, Witness

If you would like help in making your congregation a more active participant in Christ's mission, then take a look at these:

Church, Covenant, Discipleship, Election, Evangelism, Justice, Kingdom of God, Mission, Prayer, Prophets, Quietism, Reconciliation, Troublemaker, Vocation, Walk, Witness

Having doubts and reservations about Christian life and belief?

Atheism, Certitude, Faith, Revelation

Want to go deeper in your study of scripture?

Apocalyptic, Bible, Covenant, Decalogue, Election, Eschatology, Gospels, Kingdom of God, Messiah, Miracle, Parable, Prophets, Revelation

Your prayers need improvement?

Lord's Prayer, Prayer, Solitude, Spirituality, Wait

Want to strengthen your witness for social justice?

Beelzebub, Decalogue, Emigrant, Eschatology, Idolatry, Judgment, Justice, Kingdom of God, Lord, Messiah, Mission, Neighbor, Omni, Peace, Progress, Prophets, Race, Realism, Reconciliation, Riches, Sex, Sin, Truth, Unity, Wealth, Xenophobia, Zacchaeus

Want to better equip yourself as a church leader?

Body, Church, Discipleship, Evangelism, Israel, Pastor, Salvation, Solitude, Universalism, Vocation, Witness, World

The core of the Christian faith?

Atonement, Christian, Church, Covenant, Creation, Cross, Discipleship, Election, Eternal Life, Faith, God, Heaven, Holy Spirit, Incarnation, Justification, Kingdom of God, Lord, Mary, Messiah, Mission, Reconciliation, Repentant, Resurrection, Sacraments, Salvation, Savior, Trinity, Vocation, Witness

What do Christians think about when we think about death and life after death?

Death, Eschatology, Eternal Life, Heaven, Hell, Judgment, Resurrection, Salvation, Universalism

Thinking about leaving your church?

Body, Church, Eucharist, Pastor, Reconciliation, Salvation, Unity

A preacher looking for sermon help during . . .

Advent/Christmas:

Apocalyptic, Atonement, Eschatology, Incarnation, Joy, Judgment, Mary, Messiah, Peace, Prophets, Salvation, Sentimentality, Wait

Epiphany:

Certitude, Evangelism, Faith, Holy Spirit, Messiah, Mission, Preaching, Revelation, Universalism, Vocation, Walk, Witness

Lent:

Ass, Atonement, Covenant, Cross, Death, Decalogue, Discipleship, Eucharist, Exodus, Fall, Forgiveness, Holiness, Humility, Idolatry, Judgement, Justification, Messiah, Reconciliation, Repentance, Salvation, Savior, Sentimentality, Sin, Son of Man, Troublemaker, Truth, Zacchaeus

Easter:

Atonement, Certitude, Eschatology, Eucharist, Faith, Forgiveness, Heaven, Holy Spirit, Humor, Joy, Justification, Miracle, Realism, Reconciliation, Resurrection, Wait, Witness

Pentecost and Ordinary Time:

Ass, Atheism, Body, Child, Christian, Church, Covenant, Creation, Discipleship, Election, Forgiveness, Grace, Holy

Spirit, Lord's Prayer, Marriage, Mission, Neighbor, Parable, Providence, Sabbath, Sacraments, Sanctification, Spirituality, Trinity, Unity

Preparing for baptism:

Conversion, Covenant, Death, Discipleship, Election, Evangelism, Faith, Forgiveness, Holy Spirit, Race, Reconciliation, Repentance, Resurrection, Sacraments, Salvation, Sanctification, Vocation, Witness

Funeral:

Body, Covenant, Death, Eschatology, Eternal Life, Forgiveness, Heaven, Hell, Judgment, Omni, Providence, Reconciliation, Resurrection, Salvation, Savior

Wedding:

Body, Child, Covenant, Forgiveness, Love, Marriage, Sex, Solitude

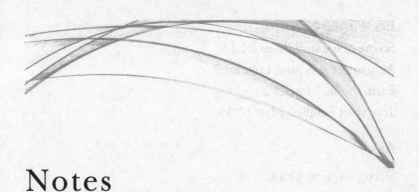

Notes

Preface

Teach us! Luke 11:1-13.

Who betrayed him. William H. Willimon, *Preachers Dare: Speaking for God* (Nashville: Abingdon, 2020).

"The Word." John 1:14.

Sacred speech. 1 Cor 4:1.

"Infinity dwindled to infancy," from Gerard Manley Hopkins, SJ (1844–1889), "The Blessed Virgin Compared to the Air We Breathe."

Thanks to Carsten Bryant, Teer Hardy, Stephen Chapman, Harriet Putman, Jeremy Begbie, Brent Strawn, and Stanley Hauerwas for help with this book.

Apocalyptic

Horned beast. Rev 13:11-14.

Night visions. Dan 7:13-28.

Taking on flesh. Ezek 37:1-14.

In Zion. Amos 6:1.

You gave to our ancestors. Neh 9:36.

Blowing of your mind! Rom 12:2.

Fall of many. Luke 1:46-51.

Secure in his stuff. Matt 24:43.

Announces it as now. Luke 10:9.

Earth shook. Matt 28:2.

Tear apart families. Matt 10:35.

Ass

Strong ass. Gen 49:14.

Asinine laity. Lev 11:26.

Neighbor's ass. Exod 20:17.

Satan and the Lord. Job 1:3.

Job with a thousand. Job 42:12.

Driver's shout. Job 39:5-8.

Balaam's. Num 22.

A donkey. Zech 9:9.

Fuzzy donkey. Matt 21:5.

The foal of a donkey. John 12:14-15; Mark 11:4.

They reply. Mark 11:7, Luke 19:30.

Atheism

Seen the Father. John 14:8

Do not see. Matt 13:13.

World to himself. 1 Cor 5:19.

Don't believe you. Sam Wells, in *In Conversation*, Samuel Wells and Stanley Hauerwas, facilitated by Maureen Knudsen Langdoc (New York: Church Publishing Incorporated, 2020), 34.

Atonement

At-one-ment. Word invented by William Tyndale for his 1526 translation of the Bible in order to translate the word that became "reconciliation."

It is finished. Matt 4:6.

Our curse. Gal 3:13.

Jesus Christ our savior. Titus 3:4-6.

Would still have come for us. Duns Scotus. William H. Willimon, *How Odd of God: Chosen for the Curious Vocation of Preaching* (Nashville: Abingdon, 2015), 27.

Sins against them. 1 Cor 5:19.

Welcome to the revolution. See N. T. Wright, *The Day the Revolution Began* (San Francisco: Harpercollins, 2018).

Baptism

Adam is put to death. Rom 3:19-22.

Begun in your baptism. William H. Willimon, *Remember Who You Are: Baptism a Model for the Christian Life* (Nashville: The Upper Room, 1998).

Beelzebub

Satan. Mark 4:15.

Devil. Luke 4:2.

Lucifer. Isa 14:12.

Of darkness. Eph 6:12.

Prince of demons. Mark 3:22.

Strong man. Luke 11:21-22.

Ruler of the air. Eph 2:1-2.

Ruler of this world. John 10:20.

Calamities to afflict Job. Job 1:13-19.

Evil since junior high. Gen 8:21, Jer 3:25.

Jumped by Satan. Luke 4:1-13.

A more acceptable time. Luke 4:13.

Has already overtaken you. Matt 12:25-28.

Recognized Jesus's identity. Matt 2:3.

Peril presented by Jesus. Luke 4:34.

Drawing all to himself. John 12:31.

Good intentions thwarted. Maybe Job 38:6-7, maybe not.

Angel of light. 2 Cor 11:14.

Noted Satan among them. Luke 22:31-32.

Groaning cosmos. Rom 8:22.

Bible

New world of the Bible. Karl Barth, "The Strange New World within the Bible," *The Word of God and the Word of Man* (New York: Harper & Brothers Publishers, 1957), 28.

Your servant is listening. 1 Sam 3:9.

From the Lord?" Jer 27:17.

Everything that is good. 2 Tim 3:16-17.

And you will find. Matt 7:7.

Named Joseph. Gen 37–42.

That talks. 2 Tim 3:16.

That you might believe. 1 John 5:13.

Body

Redemption of our bodies. Rom 8:23.

Boredom

Lives mean something. Søren Kierkegaard, *Either/Or*, translated by David F. Swenson and Lillian Marvin Swenson (Princeton, NJ: Princeton University Press, 1959), 67.

Being dull. Will Willimon, *Accidental Preacher: A Memoir* (Grand Rapids, MI: Eerdmans, 2020).

Certitude

Don't understand. G. K. Chesterton, *Orthodoxy* (San Francisco: Ignatius Press, 1995, reprint of 1908 ed.), 28.

Evening was indeed Jesus. John 20:24-29.

Good news preached to them. Matt 11:2-4.

Child

Must stoop to enter. Matt 18:1-4.

Childish things. 1 Cor 13:11.

Like this little child. Matt 18:3.

Christian

Followers of the Way. Acts 9:2.

On the way. John 14:6.

The way called Christians. Acts 11:26.

Church

He came to us. Heb 2:16-18.

Weeds growing together. Matt 13:24-31.

Saturday night. Matt 22:1-14.

Harmony with one another, NRSV; consider everyone as equal, and don't think that you're better than anyone else, CEB. Rom 12:16.

Admonish one another, NRSV; teach each other, CEB. Rom 15:14.

Wait for one another, NRSV. 1 Cor 11:33.

Build up one another, NRSV. 1 Thess 5:11.

Submit to one another, NRSV. Eph 5:21.

Forgive one another, NRSV. Col 3:13.

Pray for one another, NRSV. Jas 5:16.

Put up with one another, NRSV. Eph 4:2.

You are the Body of Christ. 1 Cor 12:27.

Appeal to the world. 2 Cor 5:20.

Count me in. Matt 18:20.

Considered to be nothing. 1 Cor 1:27-28.

Clergy

Is a priest. Exod 19:6, 1 Pet 2:9.

Conscience

Moral law within. Immanuel Kant, *Critique of Practical Reason*, 1788, translated by Thomas Kingsmill Abbott, part 2, conclusion.

Still, small voice, KJV; Thin. Quiet, CEB. 1 Kgs 9:12.

Upon us his Holy Spirit. John 20:22.

Our self-deceitful hearts. Jer 31:31-34.

Christ lives in me. Gal 2:20.

Conversion

Give you in the first place. Eph 5:14.

To inherit eternal life? Mark 10:17-31.

Covenant

Will be my people. Gen 17:8, Jer 31:33.

His brother. Gen 4.

Evil all the time. Gen 6:5.

Creation in reverse. Gen 6:7-9.

On the ark. Gen 7–8.

Give up on my creation. Gen 9:8-17.

Creation

Ambassadors in God's world. 2 Cor 5:20.

So loved the world. John 3:16.

Await redemption. Rom 8:22-24.

Not we ourselves, KJV. Ps 1 00:3.

Cross

Received him not. John 1:11.

Our violent refusal. 1 Cor 1:18.

Peter, the premier disciple. Matt 16:22.

Sinners like us. Rom 5:7.

Will save them. Mark 8:29-31, CEB.

A cliff. Luke 4:16.

They beat up on him? Matt 10:22.

Death

We fade. Ps 90:10.

Which we came. Gen 2:17.

Death is the ultimate. 1 Cor 15:26.

Deceased friend. John 11:35.

Don't want to die. Matt 26:36-46.

To kill us all. Gen 2:17.

Step nearer death. 2 Cor 4:11.

This too shall pass. 2 Cor 4:17-18.

Never to have lived. Matt 23:27.

Says Paul. Rom 3:19-22.

Die to sin. 1 Pet 2:24.

Live too. John 14:19.

Who have no hope. Rom 12:15.

Will too! John 14:19.

Decalogue

In the wilderness. Exod 7:14.

At work on Monday. Exod 5:1-5.

Discipleship

For Christ. 2 Cor 5:20.

Follow me! Matt 4:19.

Children of Israel. Acts 9:15.

Foolish and weak. 1 Cor 1:27.

Dangerous to do solo. Luke 10:1-12.

Like lightning! Luke 10:17-20.

Election

Human history. Exod 6:7; Lev 26:12; Jer 30:22. William H. Willimon, *How Odd of God: Chosen for the Curious Vocation of Preaching* (Louisville, KY: Westminster John Knox Press, 2015).

God loves you. Deut 7:7.

Faith to all nations. Isa 42:6; 49:6; 52:10; 60:3; John 8:12.

Abraham and Sarah. Gen 17.

Twelve disciples. Matt 10:1-4; Mark 3:13-19; Luke 6:12-16.

Then seventy. Luke 10:1-23.

Ends of the earth. Acts 1:8.

Will be blessed. Gen 12:3.

Mock the strong. 1 Cor 1:27.

Jesus's execution. Mark 15:6-7.

Choose the Jews. Walter Norman Ewer, journalist. Countered by Leo Rosten, American humorist, "But not so odd, As those who choose, A Jewish God, Yet spurn the Jews."

But I chose you. John 15:16.

Emigrant

Wandering Aramean. Deut 26:5.

Seeking sanctuary. Matt 2:13-21.

Strangers and immigrants, all. Eph 2:19.

Land of Egypt. Exod 23:9.

Is not our home. Heb 13:4.

Eschatology

Beginning yes of God. Exod 7:14.

Eternal Life

Resurrection. I'm life. John 11:25.

Ethics

Jump on board. See Will Willimon, *The Gospel for the Person Who Has Everything*, rev. ed. (Brewster, MA: Paraclete Press, 2020).

Eucharist

To us in bread and wine. From the poem "Christmas," by John Betjeman.

Evangelism

Come and see. John 1:39.

Letter written to the world. 2 Cor 3:3.

Be reconciled! 2 Cor 5:20.

Shine! Matt 5:14.

God's good news. Rom 1:2-4.

Where are you? Gen 3:9.

Save the lost. Luke 19:10.

Exodus

Has set us free. Gal 5:1.

Faith

Begin to make sense. Rowan Williams, *Tokens of Trust: An Introduction to Christian Belief* (Louisville, KY: Westminster John Knox Press, 2007), vii.

"I believe." John 9:35-38.

Exemplars of faith. Heb 11:8.

Their lack of faith. Mark 4:40.

Little faith. Matt 14:31.

Slow faith. Luke 24:25.

Said about him. Luke 24:25.

Seed will do. Matt 17:20.

Fall

Powerless to do it. Rom 7:22-25.

Forgiveness

Unkind and selfish. Neh 9:31; Exod 34:6; Num 14:18; Ps 86:5.

Treated us. Eph 4:32.

Father forgive. Luke 23:34.

Knew they were sinners. Luke 7:48.

Is mine, not yours. Rom 12:19.

Against us be forgiven. Mark 3:28.

To love our enemies. Matt 5:44.

Against the Holy Spirit. Matt 12:31.

Times seven. Matt 18:21-22.

Heavy lifting. Matt 18:15-17.

Merciful to me a sinner. Luke 18:13.

God

Jesus from the dead. Robert Jenson, *Systematic Theology*, vol. 1 (Oxford: Oxford University Press, 1997), 63.

God is light! 1 John 1:5.

Gospels

Else with disgust. Luke 18:9.

Healing

Tell nobody. Mark 1:40-45.

Heaven

With me in paradise. Luke 23:43.

To anyone he wants. John 17:2.

You will live too. John 14:19.

Gives the kingdom of heaven. Matt 13:31, 33, 44, 45, 47, 52; 20:21.

The future of the believer. 2 Cor 5:1-2; Phil 3:20.

Will come to judge. Rom 10:6; 1 Thess 1:10; 4:16.

Citizens of heaven. Phil 3:20.

City that is to come. Heb 13:14.

Wedding feast. Rev 19:7-10.

Innumerable multitude. Rev 7:9.

Convened by God. Heb 11:10.

With them as their God. Rev 21:1-5.

The garden. Gen 2.

New creation. 2 Cor 5:17.

No temple. Rev 21:22.

Every creature. Rev 7:9.

Holy

Sign of Israel's holiness. Gen 17:10.
Bodies as holy temples. 1 Cor 6:19-20.
Just about anywhere. John 4:21-24.
A nation of priests. Exod 19:7.
Wonderful light. 1 Pet 2:9.
Sinful man! Luke 5:8.
Holy God is descending. (cf. John 20:17).

Holy Spirit

People now do the talking. Acts 2.
What you are to say. Luke 12:11-12.
The prompting of the Holy Spirit. 1 Cor 12:3.
Well pleased, NRSV; find happiness, CEB. Mark 1:10-11.
Must test the spirits. 1 John 4:1.
Gentleness, and self-control. Gal 5:22-23.

Humility

Jesus chose humility. Phil 2:7.
Worked up by us. Mark 13:9.
Little child. Matt 18:3.
Far from the kingdom. Mark 12:34.
Some stooping. Matt 16:24-26.
Last Supper. Luke 22:24-27.
You try it. John 13:12.
Come down! Isa 64:1.

Humor

At politicians. Ps 2:4.
Angel to heal him. John 5:1-15.
Interfere with brunch. John 20:10.

Hunger

Bread alone. Deut 8:23; Matt 4:4.

Desired, took and ate. Gen 3.

Red stew. Gen 27.

Square meals a day. Exod 16:13.

What is it? Exod 16:15.

They'll be filled. Matt 5:6.

Them something to eat. Matt 14:13-21.

Feed on me! John 6:57.

Ingest all of me! John 6:54-56.

Take some wine. Luke 22:19.

Idolatry

Has its price. Rom 1.

Religious in every way. Acts 17:22.

Immortal

Final enemy. 1 Cor 15:26.

Along for the ride. 1 Cor 15:42.

Incarnation

Receive my spirit. Acts 7:59.

Is embodied in him. Col 1:19.

Assumed can't be healed. From Gregory of Nazianzus, *A Critique of Apollinarius and Apollinarianism.*

God has turned to us. John 1:14.

Face of God and live. Exod 33:20.

Israel

Wrestle all night. Gen 32:22-32.

Will be my people. Jer 30:22.

Will come to Zion. Mic 4:2.

God's faithful love. Rom 11:17-24.

Joy

God forever." The Westminster Confession of Faith. https://www
.ligonier.org/learn/articles/westminster-confession-faith/.

Joy will be complete. John 15:11.

Rejoice in the Lord always. Phil 4:4-8.

Judgment

Before Pilate. John 18:28–19:42.

Religious scholars. Luke 11:53.

Is slow to anger, NRSV. Ps 103:8.

Worship gone bad. Amos 5:21.

Changers out of the temple. John 2:13-16.

What have you been given? Matt 25:14-30.

Return on his investment. Luke 19:11-27.

Justice

Mercy kiss. Ps 85:10.

Even us, to do justice. Amos 5:24; Isa 1:17; Matt 7:12; Luke
4:10-19.

Father too. John 5:17.

Commanded to love. John 13:34.

Justification

Our God problem. 1 Cor 1:18.

Open the heavens. Matt 27:51.

Slithered into the darkness. Mark 14:50.

Heavy loads. Matt 11:28-30.

Crucify him! Luke 23:21.

Way short. Rom 3:23.

To complete the job. Phil 1:6.

Kingdom of God

It in his parables. Mark 4:26-29; Matt 13:44-46, 31-33.

Baptized are ambassadors. 2 Cor 5:20.

Listen to Matthew or Mark. Matt 13:31-32; Mark 4:30-32.

Lord

Jesus is Lord. Rom 10:9; 1 Cor 12:3.

Lord's name. Rom 10:13.

Called upon God. Joel 2:32.

Lord's Prayer

Teach us to pray. Luke 11:1.

Love

Rather than suggested love. John 13:34.

About obtaining eternal life. Mark 10:17-20.

Marriage

A wedding reception. John 2:1-12.

Remarriage after a divorce. Matt 19:9.

Matrimony in eternity. Luke 20:27-40.

Go ahead and get married. 1 Cor 7:9.

Each other in marriage. Eph 5:21-33.

Mary

Sword through her heart. Luke 2:35.
She magnified God anyway, singing. Luke 1:46-55.
To be part of it. Luke 1:26-38.

Messiah

Israel now? Acts 1:6.
One you have been expecting. Luke 7:19-23.
Says the psalm. Ps 24:1.
All Jerusalem with him. Matt 2:3.
Asked Pilate. John 18:38.
The emperor. John 19:15.
To keep quiet. Mark 8:29-30.
Be killed. Mark 8:29-31.

Miracle

Will must be done. Luke 22:42.
He could do it. John 2:1-11.
Believed in him. John 2:11.
Hungry multitude. Matt 14:13-21.
Blind see. John 9.
Lame walk. Matt 9:1-8.
Breathes again. John 11:1-44.
Good news preached. Matt 11:15.

Mission

Mine! Cornelius Van Til, see https://frame-poythress.org
/cornelius-van-til/.
May reach to the end of the earth. Isa 49:6b.
To the end of the earth. Acts 1:8.

Has come upon you. Luke 10:8-9.

From the Jews. John 4:22.

Send you. John 20:21.

Neighbor

Asked Jesus. Luke 10:25-37.

Onan

The ground. Gen 38:6-11.

Parable

Big point. Frederick Buechner, *Wishful Thinking: A Theological A
    B C* (San Francisco: Harper & Row, 1973), 66.

Parabolist Jesus. See Will Willimon, *Stories by Willimon* (Nash-
    ville: Abingdon Press, 2020), ix–xvi.

Scatter seed. Matt 13:1-16.

The catch. Matt 13:47-50.

Sling seed. Matt 13:24-30.

Of dirt? Matt 13:44-46.

One lost? Matt 18:10-14.

And more? Luke 10:25-37.

Except in parables. Mark 4:34; Matt 13:34.

Pastor

Of availability. Stanley M. Hauerwas.

Paul

World to himself. 2 Cor 5:19.

Peace

Passes understanding. Phil 4:7.
A sword. Matt 10:34.
His truth. John 14:27.

Pelagian

To do good. Rom 7:19.
Said Paul. Gal 2:20.

Prayer

To pray. Rom 8:26.
You pray. Matt 6:9; Luke 11:2.
Persistence. Luke 11:5-8; 18:1-8.
Be done. Luke 22:42.
You expected. Matt 7:7.
Of the Holy Spirit. Heb 7:25.
And persecutors. Matt 5:43-44.
Help us to pray. Rom 8:26-27.

Preaching

Us or not. Exod 17:1-7.
God's good news. Mark 1:14-18.
Preaching. Matt 4:17.
Preach good news. Luke 4:18.
Preach about ourselves. 2 Cor 4:5.
Listen to me. Luke 10:16.
And bore fruit. Matt 13:1-9.
Comes from hearing. Rom 10:17.
To frail envoys. 1 Cor 5:19.
Not return empty. Isa 55:11.

Prodigal Son

Of the prodigal son. Luke 15:11-32.

Prophets

To build and plant. Jer 1:4-10.

Bowl of fruit. Jer 24:2.

Dry bones. Ezek 37.

Smashed pots. Jer 18:1-11.

Plumb line. Amos 7:1-9.

Can but prophesy? Amos 3:8.

Unable to do it. Jer 20:9.

His royal house. Amos 7:13.

To my people Israel. Amos 7:14-15.

Providence

Not seen at the time. 1 Cor 13.

A crooked bow. Martin Luther.

The purposes of God. Rom 8:38-39.

Racism

Upon one another. Gal 3:28.

One faith, one baptism. Eph 4:5.

Realism

Without trusting it. G. K. Chesterton, *Orthodoxy* (San Francisco: Ignatius Press, 1995, reprint of 1908 ed.), 79.

Sermon on the Mount. Matt 5–7.

Reconciliation

God's up to. Rom 8:28.

Overcoming our division. Rom 8:28.

Repentance

Repent! NRSV; changed hearts and lives, CEB. Luke 3:1-14.

Showing off our goodness. Matt 6:1.

Of badness. Luke 18:13; Jas 5:16.

Do to deserve that? Luke 13:1-5.

Your life turns around. Mark 1:14-15.

Resurrection

Male disciples? Luke 24:1-12.

You're nuts. Luke 24:22.

Couldn't see. Luke 24:13-27.

Locked doors. John 20.

Breakfast on the beach. John 21:1-14.

Testimony of women. Luke 14:1-12.

Some doubted. Matt 28:17.

A gardener. John 20:15.

Resurrected Christ no hope. 1 Cor 15:17.

Hands of the living God. Heb 10:31.

Easter emotion is fear. Mark 16:8.

You always. Matt 28:20.

Tell somebody! Matt 28:10.

Revelation

And have seen him. John 14:6-7.

Blood of his cross. Col 1:19-20.

And we with God. Rev 21:3.

Waters cover the sea. Hab 2:14.

Riches

Was due to money. Matt 19:16-30.

Left everything to follow you. Matt 19:27.

Sabbath

Animals, and immigrants. Exod 20:10.

Violator of the fourth commandment. Exod 20:8-11; Matt 12:10; Mark 3:2; John 9:14-16.

Quiet sabbatical solitude. Mark 1:21-27.

God doesn't. Ps 121:4.

That benefits humanity. Mark 2:27.

Sacraments

God's gathering of God's family. 1 Cor 11:17-33.

Salvation

Save yourself and us. Luke 23:39.

Come to this house. Luke 19:1-9.

With fear and trembling. Phil 2:12.

Yes! 2 Cor 1:20.

Never heard of him. 1 Pet 3:19.

Quitting time. Matt 20:1-11.

We must be saved. Acts 4:12.

Salvation outside the church. An expression first used by Saint Cyprian of Carthage, third century.

Sanctification

In wisdom and stature. Luke 2:52.

Savior

Who is Christ the Lord. Luke 2:1.1

This who forgives sins? Luke 7:49.

For us and our salvation. From the Nicene Creed.

Sentimentality

Justify the ungodly. Rom 4:5.

Sex

Be fruitful. Gen 1:28.

No matter what. Matt 19:9.

Glorify God in your body. 1 Cor 6:19-20.

Sin

Our enemies. Matt 5:44.

All looked like reprobates. Rom 3:23.

Christ in the least of these. Matt 25:40-45.

Woman lustfully. Matt 5:28.

To be without sin. Luke 5:31.

A sinner! Luke 18:9-14.

To rebirth. John 3:3.

Jesus, that's who. Matt 5:21-22; 27-28.

But Christ in me! Gal 2:20.

Now, you try it. Luke 17:3-4.

Seventy times seven. Matt 18:21-22.

He wouldn't do, he does. Rom 7:19-25.

They're doing. Luke 23:34.

Only sinners. Rom 3:21-25.

Save sinners. 1 Tim 1:15.

Solitude

Your neighbor. Mark 12:30-31.
Except in Gethsemane. Mark 14:32-42.
As a shindig. Matt 22:1-14; Luke 15.
Let's party! Luke 15:7.
Count me in. Matt 18:20.

Son of Man or Human One

The end of history. Dan 7:13-17.
Of last judgment. Dan 7:13-14.
With great glory. Mark 13:26.

Spirituality

About me. The comedian George Carlin.
Help test the spirits. 1 John 4:1-6.
It's not the Holy Spirit. 1 Cor 13.
Spiritually deficient. Matt 5:3.

Theology

Eternal life. Luke 10:25-37.
As much as you love yourself. Deut 6:5; Lev 19:18.

Trinity

Conceived by the Holy Spirit. The Apostles' Creed.
Power of the Spirit. Luke 4:14.
And son back to us. John 14:16.

Troublemaker

The lilies. Luke 12:27-29.
Was nuts. Mark 3:21.

Upside down. Acts 17:6.

Blind fools. Matt 23:17.

Vicious wolves. Matt 7:12, 17, 23.

Righteous people but sinners. Mark 2:17.

Fire upon the earth. Luke 12:46.

Come to bring peace. Matt 10:34.

Truth

But also the truth. John 18:38.

Too cowardly to stop. John 18:38.

I am the truth. John 14:6.

Jesus loves to forgive. 1 John 1:9.

Makes us free. John 8:32.

The truth in love. Eph 4:15.

Unity

Followers might be one. John 17:21-23.

Most difficult commands. John 13:34.

Hymn to love. 1 Cor 13.

Be reconciled! Phil 4:2.

Not be all bad. 1 Cor 11:18.

Jesus continued to make community. John 19:25-27.

Universalism

Has been given all. John 3:16.

Whole world to himself. 2 Cor 5:19.

Mercy to all. All. Rom 3.

Made alive. 1 Cor 15:22.

Be saved. 1 Tim 2:4.

Father's party. Luke 15: 11-32.

Of him. Matt 25:31-46.

Bring them in too! John 10:16.

World to himself. 2 Cor 5:19.

Violence

A bit of an ear. John 18:10.

To go forth unarmed. Luke 22:51; Matt 26:52; John 18:11.

Will die by the sword. Matt 26:52.

Them to treat you. Luke 6:31.

Cheek to them as well. Matt 5:39.

The good and the bad? Luke 6:35.

"Prince." Isa 9:6.

Vocation

Through them. Matt 4:18-22.

Have commanded. Matt 28:19.

Knocked down by the risen Christ. Acts 9:1-19.

Figure out that it's God. Exod 3, 1 Sam 3.

To Gentiles and kings. Acts 9:15.

Sake of my name. Acts 9:16.

Service at the temple. Isa 6:1-13.

Living is not your own. 1 Cor 6: 19-20.

Eternal life. 1 Tim 6:12.

Fellowship with Christ. 1 Cor 1:9.

Darkness into light. 1 Pet 2:9.

Relationship with God. Rom 8:30.

Go and produce fruit. John 15:16.

Wait

God's promise. Ps 130:5.

Like eagles. Isa 40:31.

Mary and Martha. John 11:38-53.

Who wait for the morning. Ps 130:6.

Resurrection of the dead. 1 Thess 5:10; 1 Cor 15:18, 20; 1 Thess 4.

Intends you to be. 2 Cor 5:17.

To create the world. Gen 1:1–2:3.

One day of our waiting. Ps 90:4, 2; 2 Pet 3:8.

Unproductive fig tree. Luke 13:6-9.

Little Jesus. Luke 2:52.

Turn back toward home. Luke 15:20.

Possible to enjoy eternity. Rev 7:9.

Walk

In the way of trust. Rom 4:12.

That I will show you. Gen 12:1.

As the Lord told him. Gen 12:4.

Mount Moriah. Gen 22.

Who run with perseverance. Heb 12:1.

He ran. Luke 15:20.

Wealth

Big trouble. Luke 6:24.

Temptation to godlessness. Luke 12:16-21.

Due to money. Matt 19:16-30.

Travel light. Luke 10:4.

The Lamb. Rev 5:12.

Witness

To which Jesus assigns us. Acts 1:8.

Go, tell! Mark 16:7.

As witnesses. Eph 4:12-16.

Your redeemer. Attributed to Frederick Nietzsche.

Light of the world. John 8:12.

Shine! Matt 5:14.

World

To make and remake it. John 3:16.

He died for all. John 3:16.

In the world in the same way. John 13:34.

But not of the world. 1 John 2:15-17.

God intends it to be. 1 John 2:15.

Yes. 2 Cor 1:20.

No! John 1:11.

Sheep-amid-wolves dangerous. Matt 10:16.

Worship

Wonder, love, and praise. Last words of Charles Wesley's hymn, "Love Divine, All Loves Excelling," #384, *United Methodist Hymnal.*

Having turned toward us. 1 John 4:19.

Hands of a living God. Heb 10:31.

A river of righteousness. Amos 5:21-24.

I didn't know it!" Gen 28:16.

Xenophobia

Others down. Eph 2:14.

Receive him. Lev 19:34; Heb 13:2; Matt 25:35.

Called kingdom of God. Deut 10:19; Col 1:21; Rom 5:10.

Immigrated into his kingdom. John 10:16.

Membership in God's family Eph 2:19.

YHWH

Forgot God's name. Exod 3:13-14.

Who saves. Matt 1:21.

Call upon the name of the Lord. Gen 4:26.

To pray in Jesus's name. John 14:13-14.

Calls the Lord by name. Rom 10:13.

Zaccheus

Through Jericho. Luke 19:1-10.